DAISY WASHBURN OSBORN

WOMAN
WITHOUT
LIMITS

BOOKS BY DAISY AND T.L. OSBORN

BIG LOVE PLAN
FIVE CHOICES FOR WOMEN WHO WIN
THE GOOD LIFE
GOSPEL ACCORDING TO T.L. AND DAISY
HEALING THE SICK -- A LIVING CLASSIC
HOW TO BE BORN AGAIN
LIFE'S GREATEST ACHIEVEMENT
100 DIVINE HEALING FACTS
OPT FOR OPPORTUNITY
OUTSIDE THE SANCTUARY
POWER OF POSITIVE DESIRE
RECEIVE MIRACLE HEALING
RHAPSODY OF REALITIES
SEEDS TO SUCCEED
SOULWINNING -- OUT WHERE THE PEOPLE ARE
THE BEST OF LIFE
THE WOMAN BELIEVER
THERE'S PLENTY FOR YOU
TWO-WAY TOUCH
WOMAN BE FREE!
WOMEN ON BEAM -- WINNING WITH ESTEEM
WOMAN WITHOUT LIMITS
YOU ARE GOD'S BEST

For these and other titles, write to:

OSFO PUBLISHERS
Box 10, Tulsa, OK 74102

Publisher

USA WORLD HQ: BOX 10, TULSA, OK 74102

AUSTRALIA: BOX 54, GPO, SYDNEY, NSW 2001

CANADA: BOX 281, ADELAIDE ST POST STA, TORONTO, M5C 2J4

ENGLAND: BOX 148 BIRMINGHAM B3 3EQ

NEW ZEALAND: BOX 3442, GPO, WELLINGTON

DEDICATION

To women and girls around the world who constitute the female part of the body of Christ; to the daughters of God's royal family who are created in His own image and for whom He has paid the supreme price to redeem and to restore to His side as partners with Him, ministering love in a hurting world.

DAISY MARIE WASHBURN OSBORN

Bible Quotations in this book have been personalized, and sometimes synopsized, to encourage individual application. They are derived from The New King James Version and the Living Bible unless otherwise noted.

The Author

ISBN 0-87943-076-1

Copyright 1990 by Daisy Washburn Osborn

Printed in the United States of America

All Rights Reserved

Most Osborn books and cassettes are available at quantity discounts for bulk purchase to be used for gifts, resale, ministry outreaches, educational or other purposes.

For details write:

OSFO Publishers
Box 10
Tulsa, OK 74102 USA

CONTENTS

Introduction

By T.L. Osborn

THE GENERAL IDEA of the Christian message is that it is good news for people in need.

Whether that good news is given by a woman or by a man, to an individual or to a crowd, in a house or in a temple, is irrelevant to the issue.

The usual concept of Christian ministry is to do good to people, to help and lift and heal and save humanity.

Whether such action is taken by a believing woman or by a believing man, reaching out to one person or to one thousand persons, at a table in a private house or from a podium in a park, is insignificant to the matter.

The assumption in Christian motivation is that unsaved people need to be rescued; that lost people need to be found. Whether such rescue is undertaken by a man or by a woman, affecting one person or a dozen or a hundred people, privately or publicly, is by all logistics, immaterial to the operation.

Distorted Logistics

Suppose a crowded hotel is burning. A few men are struggling to save those whom they can reach. Due to limited equipment and personnel, it is evident that over half of those trapped will be burned to death.

A group of community-minded women arrive
with additional mobile equipment which they have
managed to commandeer; power ladders, hoses,
smoke masks and resuscitation gear, plus their
willing muscle-power and professional expertise in
fire-fighting and evacuation procedures.

Enter the august clergy.

With Ben Franklins perched on noses, antique
parchments in hand, bedecked in clerical collars and
priestly robes, pious fingers are thrust heavenward
as their canting voices implore:

"Women, halt your rescue!

"We are priests of ancient heritage.

"Sacred tradition holds that you are not permitted to act in the public rescue of fire victims!

"Certified orthodoxy mandates that your place is
in the home, in silence and in submission!

"Your intrusion here is not sanctioned by the
venerable church fathers.

"Better that the people burn to death than that
women infringe on man's ordained mission of sav-
ing lives!"

As ridiculous as that may sound, a very recent
fundamental church conference passed a long reso-
lution about *Women's Role in the Church and Home*
in which they affirmed "their adherence to the New

Testament teaching that women are not legitimate candidates for ordination and that God has committed to men the important responsibility of leadership and authority in the church and in the home."

Scores of similar rules, resolutions and regulations, adopted during recent years, could be cited here.

Untenable Restraints for Women

The pulpit, the press and the media have combined to impose increasingly stringent and rigid prohibitions for women, restraining them from public ministry in the church. These discriminating injunctions depict a kind of female-dominance phobia in much contemporary church leadership.

Dr. Adam Clarke, one of the most eminent of traditional Bible scholars, comments about the non-rational theory of keeping women silent in the church today.

He says of 1Co. 14:34:   "It is the only one verse in the whole Book of God which even by a false translation can be made prohibitory of female speaking in the Church.

Then Dr. Clarke asks: "How comes it then, that by this one isolated passage, which according to our best Greek authorities, is wrongly rendered and wrongly applied, woman's lips have been sealed for centuries, and the *testimony of Jesus, which is the spirit of prophecy*[1] has been silenced (in women)? How is it, that this solitary text has been allowed to stand, unexamined and unexplained?"

Dr. Clarke asks, "How can it be that learned commentators who have known its true meaning, have upheld the delusion, and enforced it as a divine precept binding upon all female disciples through all times?"

Then Dr. Clarke concludes: "Surely there must have been some unfaithfulness, *craftiness* and *handling the word of life deceitfully*[2] somewhere. These divines and commentators have involved themselves in all sorts of inconsistencies and contradictions; and worse, they have nullified some of the most precious promises of God's word."[*]

No Legitimate Limits

I can find no proof in God's redemptive plan that a woman is any more limited in Christ's ministry than a man is.

I see no Biblical evidence that a woman has any less value to God in public Christian ministry than a man, or that a woman should be any more restrained or repressed in sharing the Gospel with hurting humanity than a man.

I see no reason to imply that the promises, the teachings, and the commands of Christ are not addressed to women exactly the same as they are to men.

I see no indication that the gifts and power of

---

[*]*The Magna Charta of Woman*, By Jessie Penn-Lewis, page 33-34.

the Holy Spirit are to function any more limited, or
any less effectively in a woman's life than in a
man's.

I see nothing in Christ's ministry or in the
Book of Acts to indicate any difference in the value
or status or activities or effectiveness of one sex
over the other.

Christ places no more limits on the ministry of
women who follow Him, than He does on that of
men who follow Him.

A Changing World

Bible believing women around the world are
awakening to their unlimited position in the body of
Christ and to their equality in God's redemptive
plan for human persons.

In this book, Daisy is reaching out to God's
woman, in any culture, of any race, in any nation,
with Biblical encouragement and enlightenment. She
is helping women to discover that there are no legitimate limits in public or private Christian ministry for those who follow Christ as His representatives to people.

What Motivated This Book

Daisy had an overwhelming experience in which
Jesus appeared to her and told her to *"Preach the
gospel to women."*

We knew that Christ could not be true to His
own gospel and limit Daisy's commission to women,
because the gospel is for *every creature*.   For a

woman to preach only to women would be as unbalanced as it would be for men to preach only to men.

Daisy understood Christ's words to her: *"Be one who includes women when you preach the gospel. Address the gospel to women too. Do not ignore them. The gospel is for women the same as it is for men, so SAY SO! Preach the gospel to women the same as to men. Include the women!"*

Therefore, this book is addressed to women. But it is for men too. It is addressed to women because almost no other gospel book is directed to them — or even includes them, unless specifically referring to women.

Even women preachers and authors address their messages to "man" and to "men." They talk about their "spirit-man." They say that "God needs a man;" that "God loves man;" that "man must be saved." Usually women are not even mentioned.

Daisy includes women when she preaches the gospel because Jesus paid the same redemptive price for women as He paid for men. The dignity of a woman's personhood and her value to God merits inclusion in gospel presentation.

I encouraged Daisy to produce this book. I encourage every woman to read it and to discover her equality, her identity, her dignity and her destiny in God's redemptive plan for humankind. And I encourage every man to read it for the same reason.

1.   Re.19:10
2.   2Co.4:2

Preface

TRICKS, TRENDS AND TRADITIONS

THE STATUS OF WOMEN and their roles in life have changed from one epoch to another.

A new day has dawned for women as they learn to recognize and to esteem their equality, the dignity of their own personhood, and their own divine purpose in God's redemptive plan.

Formidable changes are being affected by thinking women in the worlds of science, of medicine, of politics, of industry, of enterprise, of the arts, *etc.* Women have proven to be unlimited in all of these fields.

Why has a woman's place in public Christian ministry been so restricted?

Why should Christian women be hampered and handicapped by archaic religious dogmas and ecclesiastical restraints which are as outdated as a tin wash tub and a clothes line in an epoch of pushbutton washers and driers?

In the light of woman's economic, academic, political and legal emancipation, can scholarly, professional women allow themselves to be repressed, silenced and limited in God's service and ministry by two brief Pauline statements,[1] interpreted out of their cultural context?

If the restraints inferred upon women in the
church were intended by Paul to apply to female
believers of all ages, as is dogmatized by traditional theology, they would indeed contradict the
whole of New Testament redemptive teaching as
revealed and taught by Paul.

Is woman an inferior creation of God, destined
for subordination and second class citizenship in
His family and in His Church?

Does the redemption of Christ include women
the same as men? To a different degree? Or is
it limited according to gender?

The salvation of Christ, in its fullest extent, is
offered to women the same as it is to men. Is
salvation an experience that is limited according to
the gender of the recipient?

Since Eve first partook of the forbidden fruit,
are women justified before God, through Christ,
from all sins — except that one?

Is justification from all sins available to men,
but is it limited for the women?

A woman can be born again through faith in
Christ the same as a man. Are the effects of that
new birth limited according to a person's gender?

Jesus Christ came to seek and to save women
the same as men. Are women saved in a more
limited sense than men?

The Great Commission of Christ is intended
for His women disciples the same as for His men

disciples. Is a woman disciple limited in how she may serve her Lord because she is female?

The promises of Christ are intended for women as well as for men. Is their fulfillment limited for women because of their gender?

The Holy Spirit is promised to women believers the same as to men believers. Is the Holy Spirit to be limited in women according to restricted female roles in God's service? Does His expression depend upon the gender of the believer?

Is God in a woman to be subordinated to God in a man?

Women believers receive power to witness of Christ after the Holy Spirit comes upon them, the same as men believers do. Is the Holy Spirit's power to witness of Christ to be limited or silenced in women believers — especially in public?

Was it God's plan for women followers of Christ to be active in ministry as His witnesses only during the few years of the Early Church before a man named Paul would be converted, and would allegedly instruct women not to do the things Christ had commissioned them to do?

Jesus Christ expected women who received Him as Lord to obey Him. But did He plan later for them to acquiesce in favor of Paul's alleged position for women to be silent?

The lives and ministries of early Christian women and men are examples for Christian women

and men to emulate today. Were they not all commanded to receive the Holy Spirit?

Were they not all together *with the women,* and
in one accord? Were they not *all filled* with the
Holy Spirit and did they not all *begin to speak ... the
wonderful works of God;* the *sons and the daughters,*
the *servants and the handmaidens?* Should it be
different today?

*Believers were the more added to the Lord, mul-
titudes both of men and women.*[2] Obviously both the
men and the women were obeying Christ, witnessing
of Him by the power of the Holy Spirit which they
had *all* received — the women the same as the men.

Under the *great persecution,* they were *all
scattered abroad.*[3] They all (both men and women)
went *everywhere preaching the word. (v.4)* Is it
any wonder therefore that Saul, the persecutor,
*dragged off both men and women, committing them to
prison? (v.3).*

Should women today not emulate those early
women believers who received the Holy Spirit and
who became public witnesses of Christ *to the
uttermost part of the earth* as Christ commissioned?

The real fruits of the Spirit are to be evident
in the lives of women believers the same as they
are in the lives of men believers.

Authentic spiritual fruits are not limited in a
believing woman's life according to the roles cast
by her cultural environment. If they were, would
those be the genuine fruits of the Spirit? Spiritual
fruits are not measured by gender?

The real gifts of the Spirit are to be manifested in a spirit-filled woman's life the same as they are in a spirit-filled man's life.

Authentic spiritual gifts are not limited in a woman because she is female. If they were, would they be the true gifts of the Spirit? True spiritual gifts do not have sexist attributes.

The life of Jesus Christ makes a woman a new creature the same as it does a man. Is that life of Christ limited, restrained, or restricted in a woman because of her gender? And if so, is it the divine life of Christ? Christ's life is not sexist?

Is the ministry of Jesus expressed through women any less effectively than it is through men? If so, is it Christ's ministry that is expressed? Christ's ministry cannot be equated sexually?

Jesus Christ is the same yesterday and today and forever, in and through a woman believer the same as He is in and through a man believer.

Is Jesus limited in His expression through a woman? Is He expressed by gender? The love of God is to be represented through women Christians the same as it is through men Christians.

The nature of Christ is to be reflected through women who receive Him the same as it is through men who receive Him. Is His nature limited in a woman because she is female? Does the expression of His nature depend upon gender?

WOMEN'S NATIONAL CONFERENCE — E. AFRICA

Daisy Osborn seeds the women of the world in her national women's mass rallies abroad.

INDONESIAN WOMEN'S DAY — SURABAJA

WOMEN'S NATIONAL MIRACLE DAY — KAMPALA

AUSTRALIAN CONFERENCE

A woman can consecrate herself to Christ and to His service the same as a man can. Both women and men can speak out for their Lord and bear private and public testimony of His mercy to them. Must women who love their Lord be excluded from giving public witness of His grace and power in their lives?

It is time for believing women to question unreasonable traditions which contradict redemptive principles and which obstruct redeemed women from the gospel ministries for which Christ has called them.

Jesus Christ indicated no such limitations for women who followed Him in Bible days, nor has He ever implied any such restraints upon women who follow Him today.

1.   1Co.14:34-35   2.   Ac.5:14
      1Ti.2:11-12   3.   Ac.8:1

Foreword

INCLUSIVE REDEMPTION

THE WHOLE BODY of biblical redemptive truth teaches divine justification and restoration from sin for *whoever believes.*[1] The Bible declares full salvation and divine righteousness for every person, regardless of sex, race, social status or color, who receives Christ.

God's Word makes it clear that every believer may receive the power of the Holy Spirit, whether male or female, and it encourages all Christians, regardless of sex or race, to imitate Christ in loving service and in ministry to people.

The Gospels and the Book of Acts are replete with examples of women in ministry, speaking, prophesying and serving people, as God's co-laborers. They were never limited in ministry in ways dictated by traditional male theologians.

Paul's brief statements, *I do not permit a woman to teach*[2] and *let your women keep silent in the churches*[3] have been extracted out of their cultural context, distorted in their meaning and significance, and held up before women as arbitrary barricades, obstructing them from public ministry in the church for centuries.

These statements and their original intent were relevant to the issues concerning women of that medieval epoch, and particularly to women converts from pagan religions who were being integrated into the new Judeao Christian communities. But they were never intended as dogmas to prevent or to limit women in Christian ministry for all times.

Paul's counsel: *Let your women keep silent in the churches,they are not permitted to speak ... as the law also says*[4] cannot refer to the Mosaic law since nowhere in Old Testament scriptures is the subject dealt with.

Rather, Paul's words were almost an exact quote from the Jewish oral law in the Talmud which states: "It is a shame for a woman to let her voice be heard among men."

God's law never inferred such a prohibition upon women. It was Rabbis who stipulated that restraint. Paul, a learned Jew, was quoting from rabbinical rules and dogmas which greatly influenced early Church teaching, but which were never God's word of limitation upon women for all times.

The famed Jessie Penn-Lewis says that these ancient restraints upon Christian women are "because three passages in the epistles of Paul have been rendered into English in a way that they have entirely misinterpreted the teaching of the Apostle, and by doing so have shut out women from proper and dignified work in the church of God..." She adds: "Christian women have been robbed of their true status in the church because translators, and many expositors, have failed to perceive the true setting of the apostle's words." *

The Magna Charta of Woman, By Jessie Penn-Lewis, pages 21, 24.

Mrs. A.J. Gordon, wife of the renowned Bible expositor, encourages women to adopt the attitude toward Christian ministry that was expressed in *2S.15:15* As your servant, I am *ready to do whatever my Lord the King may appoint.* She writes that in *the last days*[5] significant changes would be affected by God's Spirit:

1) Both *sons* and *daughters* would *prophecy.*

2) Spiritual gifts and talents would be given to *servants* and *handmaidens* alike.

3) *Whoever should call upon the name of the Lord would be saved.*

4) *Jews and Greeks, bond and free,* rich and poor, *men and women* could receive the gift of salvation.

Paul says that the new Jesus-community is *neither Jew nor Greek, neither slave nor free, neither male nor female; for you are all one in Christ Jesus.*[6]

Hundreds of scholarly volumes have clarified statements by Paul about women, and the customs involved at the time.

Rather than to "re-invent the wheel" by re-expounding what reputed Bible scholars have elucidated so thoroughly, I encourage women to follow Jesus and to obey His directives. *He* is Lord, and *His* words are what count most.

Even if Paul's remarks about restricting women in ministry were intended to conform women of all times to the cultural standards of that medieval epoch, I would still encourage women to obey the Lord Jesus. Why should women defer to the discipline of someone who was not even converted until years after Christ's commission to His followers. Paul asks: *Was I crucified for you? Were you baptised in my name?*[7] He urged, *Imitate me* (only) *as I imitate Christ.*[8]

Are the cultural restraints upon females of a bygone epoch relevant today? Should Roman or Greek or pagan laws of an ancient civilization be imposed upon women today?

What is vital to believing women today is what Jesus Christ taught *all* of His followers to do, what His attitude toward women was, and what His redemption means to every believer now. These issues never concern one's gender any more than one's race.

Jesus Christ and His life and ministry are totally relevant to women today. He is unlimited in the woman who has received Him by faith.

There is unlimited potential for every woman believer to be Christ's follower, His ambassador, His representative, and His co-worker in whatever capacity she may be inspired or led or called by Him to serve?

1.   Jn.3:16;   2.   1Ti.2:12   6.   Ga.3:28
      Ac.10:43;   3.   1Co.14:34   7.   1 Co.1:13
      Ro.10:13;   4.   1Co.14:34   8.   1 Co.11:1
      1Jn.5:1   5.   Ac.2:17;
                             He.1:2

Prologue

MY WITNESS

I AM A WOMAN believer in Christ.

I decided early in life to embrace Him as my Lord and Master. I committed my life to His service, to follow and to imitate Him as well as I could. I chose to receive His Holy Spirit in my life and to allow Him full control.

I believed, from my conversion, that my life as a Christian was to represent Jesus to people and to allow Him to carry on His ministry through me.

I understood that I, as a lady, was Christ's teammate, and I was never influenced to believe that He limited His life and ministry through me because of my gender.

In my high school years, I was active in my church and I was successful. At the young age of 17, I married T.L. Osborn, an evangelist, and immediately I became an equal partner with him as God led us into a successful world missionary and mass evangelism ministry.

When I was only nineteen, we co-founded a new church and I shared all pastoral duties from the pulpit to the class room, on an equal basis with my husband.

I chose to be a loving wife, a partner in our home, a friend and a teammate with my husband.

When children graced our marriage, I became a good mother and my husband became a good father. Both of our lives had to be greatly adapted to parenthood, but those new roles never affected or diminished our status as ministers of the gospel.

When I became a mother, my husband became a father. But both of us continued to be full time gospel ministers and pastors.

At the young ages of 20 and 21, we became missionaries in India — both of us. Neither of us was limited in ministry because of our gender. We were both called of God, commissioned by Christ, ordained and sent forth by our missions board to teach and to preach Jesus Christ.

After returning to the USA with a greater concern for our world than ever, we both prayed and fasted for God's direction toward greater success in His work.

Jesus Christ appeared to each one of us — at different times and in distinct ways. We were each re-confirmed by Him, and we both re-committed our lives to His service among the unreached peoples of our world.

Since those experiences, we have ministered the gospel for more than four decades, conducting great public crusades in stadiums, ball parks, race courses and on fields, in over seventy nations. Audiences have consistently numbered from 20,000 to 250,000 in each meeting.

In our follow-up Bible teaching seminars, and in conferences and conventions worldwide, we have both taught and shared with tens of thousands of Christian workers — women, as well as men, helping them to discover their own identity, equality, dignity, and destiny in God's redemptive plan.

My husband and I co-founded our world headquarters church at Tulsa, Oklahoma, the *International Gospel Center*. As a pastoral team we shared equally all aspects of the church ministry — the teaching, the preaching, the counseling, the consecrations, laying on of hands, ordinations, weddings, funerals, commissions, serving the holy communion, *etc.*

I have never been limited in Christian ministry because I am a woman, nor is our daughter, Rev. LaDonna Osborn who is the pastor of *International Gospel Center*, nor are hundreds of other women ministers whom I know.

I would never permit a few words by Paul, spoken to women of an archaic epoch, to limit my obedience to my Lord in my generation.

He has chosen me as one of His commissioned ambassadors, to represent Him and to share His message any place, or in any circumstance, or to any individual, or to any multitude, or in any church, or in any convention, or on any field in the whole world.

Jesus Christ is the One who has saved me, called me and commissioned me. It is He who sent His Spirit upon me, enduing me with His power. He has authorized me to use His name, to proclaim His message, and to be His witness.

Paul said concerning those *who are the called
according to His purpose,* that *whom He foreknew,
He also predestined ... and whom He predestined,
these He also called; and whom He called, these He
also justified; and whom He justified, these He also
glorified.*[1]

These facts are as true for women believers
who obey Christ in loving service, as they are for
men believers who obey Him.

As women, we can ask with Paul: *What shall
we say to these things? If God is for us, who can be
against us?* v.31 *Who shall lay anything to the
charge of* (women as) *God's elect? Is it not God
who justifies* (us)? v.33 *Who is he who condemns*
(women as unworthy for public ministry)? *It is
Christ who died* (for us) ... *that is risen again, who
... makes intercession for us.* v.34

It is our Lord Jesus Christ who has made me a
Woman Without Limits, and He wills to do the
same for any woman who feels the desire or call
to His service.

In reverence to my Lord and in obedience to
His authority in my life, I shall never acquiesce to
patriarchal dogmas or to biased theological pronouncements which would demean my personhood as
a woman created in God's image, or that would
circumscribe me, or deprecate me, or limit me in
representing my Lord to any individual or to any
multitude, in any form of ministry to which I felt
He has inspired or led or called me.

I was born a female. I was re-born a
Christian. A Christian is not characterized by gen-

der. In Christ there is no difference.

Religion has traditionally limited women. God does not. Jesus does not. The Holy Spirit does not. God's Word does not. My life is the proof, and it is my hope that this book, *Woman Without Limits*, will encourage every woman who reads it to discover her unlimited potential in her ministry of love to a hurting world, as a friend and as a partner with Christ.

1   Ro.8:28-30

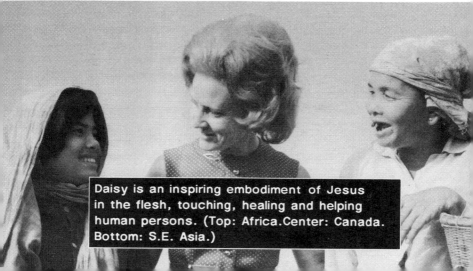

Daisy is an inspiring embodiment of Jesus in the flesh, touching, healing and helping human persons. (Top: Africa. Center: Canada. Bottom: S.E. Asia.)

PART I

YOUR
RICH
HERITAGE

ONCE YOU HAVE BEEN converted, you as a woman *become a daughter of God. Jn.1:12* You belong to His family, recreated in His image. You are inter-linked with deity.

God did not make womankind inferior. You are first class all the way. He created you unique. You are exceptional, one of a kind.

This book will help you to recognize the value God places on you and the limitless potential within you. It will inspire you to discover your rich heritage and your own possibilities.

In Christ, there is salvation, dignity and self-esteem for women; not religious servitude or inferiority.

In Him, there is deliverance and significance for womankind; not acquiescence or meaningless mediocrity.

No one created in God's image needs to respect archaic dictums or pronouncements made in the name of God, of the Church or of tradition, by one who presumes superiority over women by relegating them to a subordinate status in life.

Every woman on earth has unlimited possibilities in God. Redemption is not qualified racially or sexually. Every human person can become a new creature in Christ and can become His co-worker and representative to the world.

Chapter 1

GOOD NEWS FOR WOMEN

IT IS VITAL that you, as a woman, accept your true identity with God.

The concept you have of yourself, of your value and of your purpose in life is the very core of your personality. A strong self-image is the best possible preparation for success.

This book will help you to recognize the value God places on you and the limitless potential within you. It will inspire you to discover your rich heritage and your own possibilities.

A Dallas businesswoman said, "You are somebody because God never wastes His time to make a nobody."

God loves you like you are and has paid for every wrong you ever committed. That is what He wants you to know, and He believes in you so much that He thinks you will respond positively to Him, as you discover your rich heritage.

The French Prince

King Louis XVI of France was beheaded, along with the queen, during the French Revolution.

Then they prepared to guillotine the little prince. But the mob yelled, "Don't kill him. He is so young that his soul will go to heaven. That is too good for his father's son."

They said, "Give the lad to the witch. She
will teach him to curse, then when he dies, he will
go to hell."

The witch tried, but the prince would stomp his
feet and say, "No! I will not curse! I was born to
be a king and I cannot speak that way."

When you discover the value God places on you,
you will know that your heritage is too great to
ever be compromised.

A black woman in the South asked, "How can I
be inferior, when I am a child of God?"

Identity for Greatness

This book is good news for you. There is no
condemnation in it. Jesus did not come to condemn
anyone. Neither do I. *God did not send His Son
into the world to condemn the world, but that the
world through Him might be saved.*[1]

This book will lift you because it is based on
good news. No one has the right to speak or to
write in a way to demean, to degrade or to dishonor womanhood.

Every woman, regardless of her race, her rank
or her record deserves respect and esteem as one
for whom Jesus Christ laid down His life in love.
God has created no second class human persons, no
one inferior, insignificant or subservient in His
family.

The same Lord over all is rich to all who on Him. [2]

For whoever — women as well as men, calls on the name of the Lord shall be saved. [3]

For you are all the children of God ... There is neither Jew nor Greek, there is neither bond nor free, there is neither male nor female; for you are all one in Christ Jesus. [4]

1.   Jn.3:17
2.   Ro.10:12
3.   Ro.10:13
4.   Ga.3:28

Daisy ministers at National Women's Conference — USA

Daisy preaches at Mission Convention — Norway

Daisy teaches at National Women's Congress — Uganda

Chapter 2

CREATED LIKE GOD

A YOUNG LADY in Europe traveled to Tulsa, Oklahoma, to talk to my husband and me.

Her parents had told her that she was stupid and unattractive.

Dominated by such a negative, destructive atmosphere, she became insecure and withdrawn. She was afraid to go out on the streets alone. She scrubbed floors to gain a subsistence in life.

She was not dull witted, but was simply an emotional human casualty. She had been mentally devastated by calloused parents who transferred their own self-contempt to the closest victim they could reach — their own daughter.

Love Power in Action

We took that young lady into our private prayer room, and showed her love, esteem and compassion. Behind her emotionally scarred face was a lovely lady who wanted to be somebody. She desperately seized each statement that lifted her self-esteem like a drowning person grasps a straw.

Her mouth and her face twitched uncontrollably as she talked. Her head and her shoulders twisted involuntarily. Her whole body reflected her emotional devastation.

One may have judged her to be a neurotic psychopath, yet her essential problem derived from the barrage of ugly negative words by her own parents. They had mutilated the self-image of their daughter with the derogatory words they had deluged her with.

The New Confession

During our prayer, as tears rolled down her cheeks, we asked her to confess out loud:

> I am created in God's likeness. I am
> somebody important in God's eyes. He
> believes in me. He loves me and needs me.
> I am part of His plan. God loves me just
> as He loves everyone else.

Repeatedly we prayed with her, and when she returned to Europe, she was a new woman. She believed that she had a purpose for living and that she could succeed in life with God, because she had a new outlook. Her whole life would change because her thoughts were changed.

The Battered Beaten Penny

Just before she left, T.L. and I were on the jog trail alongside the river in Tulsa, and we saw in the street a battered, beaten penny, scarred by the hundreds of vehicles that had rolled over it.

The Lord impressed T.L.: "That coin is worth as much as a beautiful, new penny. It is like that dear lady from Europe.

"Go tell her what I have said to you. Though

she is scarred and battered by those who have
demeaned her, tell her that she is as valuable as
any lady in Europe."

We took that coin and placed it in her hands,
giving her God's message.   While she held it, she
repeated:

> "My life is like this battered coin. But
> I am as valuable as the most beautiful
> lady in Europe!"

She promised to keep that coin with her Bible,
and every time anyone said anything derogatory to
her, she resolved that she would hold it and say:

> "My life is like this battered coin. But
> I am as valuable as the most beautiful
> lady in Europe!"

She Discovered Her Value

She discovered the facts that gave her self-
esteem.   She is God's creation. He loves her and
paid the supreme price to redeem her back to Him
so that she and God could be at one, could walk together and could share life as He planned for her.

That is what He planned for every woman, and
it is He who caused me to prepare this book for
you, so that you can discover who you really are.

That discovery will actually start the miracle
you need in life. Problems will be solved. Sicknesses will go away. Fear and apprehension will
disappear.   Guilt will be gone. Insecurity will
vanish. You will begin rising up on the inside.

Daisy and T.L., her husband, have shared
equally in their ministries to millions
in over seventy nations, spanning more
than four decades of successful gospel
outreaches to the world.

Daisy is received by the Honorable President of the Republic of Kenya. (Above) She reads to him a special letter from T.L., her husband, and (below) shows His Excellency a large panoramic photo of over a quarter-million people attending the Osborn crusade in Uganda where he had helped to negotiate political stability.

Destiny Is Now at Work in You

Why were you chosen for this information which has lifted tens of thousands of women around the world?

It is God's way of saying: "I love you. I created My best when I created you. I paid a price for you and you are worth all that I ever paid for you. I have destined My best for you."

Right now, say to yourself:

"I am created in the image of God, to be like Him, to manifest Him in human form. I am made for life and love, for power and prosperity, for success and progress, for dignity and achievments."

As you respond to these facts and believe that you have unique value and purpose, you are planting the seeds of truth in your life which guarantee the kind of harvest you will reap.

God did not make woman inferior. You are first class all the way. He created you unique. You are exceptional, one of a kind.

Before you were born, you existed in God's mind. He knew this world would need you. He planned you with a special purpose that no one but you could fulfill.

Chapter 3

GOD AND YOU

GOD NEVER PLANNED for any woman to become a non-achiever or a failure in life.

No woman was ever intended for prostitution or infidelity, for neglect or shame, for sickness or suffering, for destructiveness or nonproductivity.

No woman was ever destined by God to crawl in shame or to cower in a subservient role.

Mary Magdalene is a vivid example. Jesus saw in her the strength of her resolve to believe in Him, even when the men retreated in seclusion, after His crucifixion. They were afraid and were filled with unbelief. But Christ saw Mary's qualities. Others only saw her past problems and her record as a demon possessed woman. No wonder it amazed the disciples when Mary Magdalene was the one who brought them the news that Christ had risen and that she had *seen the Lord, and she gave them His message.*[1]

There are no limits for a woman who follows Christ.

The Dream That God Esteems

Accept yourself as a woman created in God's image, made to be like Him.

David said in Psalm 8:5, *God has made you a*

little lower than the angels (original Hebrew: *a little lower than God*).   Can you see yourself as a woman in God's class of being?

You may be down on yourself, but God values and esteems you.

You may condemn yourself or allow others to discredit you, but God only wants to lift you up. See yourself in His image.

Realize that no woman was ever created to be poor, unhappy, dominated, manipulated, abused, shamed or walked on.

God designed you for His abundance, for His nobility, for His kingdom.   Nothing can stop or limit you, once you discover your rich heritage.

1.   Jn.20:18 LB

Chapter 4

GOD'S PLAN – NO LIMITS

ADAM AND EVE were created by God, then placed in the Garden of Eden which He had planted for them.[1]

Both were made in God's own image, to plan and to work with Him, carrying out His ideas on earth.[2]

Then temptation came.[3] Both the woman and the man sinned by doubting God's word. Separated from God's presence,[4] they became the slaves of Satan whom they believed and obeyed. They forfeited their self-esteem, self-worth and their inheritance of life and dignity with God.

God never abandoned His dream of having them both near Him. But being righteous, He could not condone their sin.[5] His law could not be moderated. *The soul that sins shall die.*[6]

Adam and Eve engendered sin in all of the human race which was their offspring. All sinned, so all must die. But God wanted all to live, so He found a way to redeem us all and to justify us and to restore us to Him.

One who was innocent could take the place of the guilty and die as their substitute. Since no crime could be punished twice, once the punishment was suffered by a willing substitute, the crime of the guilty would be paid for, and the guilty would be justified as though she or he had never sinned.[7]

Jesus Christ, God's Son, was perfect.[8]   He had never sinned.[9]   He came and took on Himself the sins of the whole world and suffered the full penalty for the sins of all people.[10]

God so loved the world that He gave His only begotten Son, that whoever believes in Him should not perish but have everlasting life.[11]

All that would ever be required of woman or of any man, to receive total justification before God, is that you simply believe that Jesus Christ died in your place, that He endured the judgment and suffered the penalty for all of your sins, and that you respond to His love by willingly confessing your faith in Him to others.[12]

Doing that, an incredible miracle takes place: *God took the sinless Christ and poured into Him your sins.   Then, in exchange, He poured God's goodness into you.*[13]

Jesus Christ became the way back to God for every woman and for every man who believes in Him.

Christ removed forever the condemnation of your sins and dissolved the barrier between you and God, so that you are now welcome to return to His presence where you can once again share His lifestyle.[14]   You have been restored to the dignity and righteousness of God for which He originally created you.   You have been justified — as though you had never sinned.

Restored to God

Once you as a woman — or as a man, understand that your sins separated you from God, but that He loved you too much to leave you to die in your sins; once you believe that Jesus Christ died in your place; once you repent of your sins and accept Jesus as your Savior and receive Him and His life in you, then you are regenerated, you are saved, you are redeemed, you are born again, and you receive His new kind of life in you.

When this miracle comes to pass, you are a new creature in Christ Jesus, and you as a woman, must never again allow yourself or anyone else to condemn, discredit or demean what God has paid so much to redeem and to justify.

Once you accept God's forgiveness and believe that the life of Jesus Christ is imparted to you, you esteem your value as a royal daughter in the kingdom of God; you perceive a new image of yourself as a friend, a co-laborer, a partner and a teammate with God, unlimited, uninhibited and unrestrained in any capacity of personal or public ministry to which you feel inspired or led or called by Him to serve.

1.	Ge.2:8	7.	Ro.5:1	10.	Jn.1:29
2.	Ge.1:26-31	8.	He.5:9		1Pe.2:24
3.	Ge.3:1-6	9.	2Co.5:21		2Co.5:21
4.	Ge.3:22-24		He.4:15	11.	Jn.3:16
5.	Is.59:1-3		He.7:26	12.	Ro.10:9-10
6.	Eze.18:4,20		1Pe.1:19	13.	2Co.5:21LB
	Ro.5:12		1Pe.2:22	14.	He.10:18-22

"The new birth is a miracle. When you stop seeing yourself as inferior, then you begin to believe in others. Discover the exciting facts about your rich heritage."

Chapter 5

DISCOVER THE NEW LIFE

ONCE YOU HAVE BEEN converted, you become a daughter of God.[1] You belong to His family, recreated in His image. You are inter-linked with deity.

If you are in Christ, you are a new creation; old things have passed away; behold, all things have become new.[2]

The new birth is a miracle. You are made new. Believe in that change. Think about it, confess it, sing about it, live like the changed person that you are when you embrace Christ in your life.

When you stop seeing yourself as inferior, then you will stop seeing others as inferior. As you start believing in yourself, then you will begin to believe in others.

To become a *Woman Without Limits* as God designed you to be, here are nine facts for you to discover concerning your rich heritage:

1. DISCOVER that God created you as a woman, to be like Him.[3]

2. DISCOVER that when sin entered the human family through Adam and Eve,[4] God did not want you as a woman, to die for your sins,[5] though His law prescribed that *the wages of sin is death.*[6]

3. DISCOVER that He loved you as a
woman, too much to let you die.[7] He gave
His Son to assume all of the legal punishment for your sins.[8]

4. DISCOVER that Jesus suffered the punishment for your sins, in your place, and that
therefore you as a woman, are free from all
guilt and all judgment forever.[9]

5. DISCOVER that God paid the supreme
price to redeem you as a woman to Himself,
in order to prove how much He wants to
share His life with you.[10]

6. DISCOVER that since the price of your
redemption is paid in full by the life and the
blood of Jesus Christ,[11] you as a woman,
are free, you are no longer guilty, and you
can never be judged or condemned again for
your sins which have been expunged forever.[12]

7. DISCOVER that since there is nothing to
separate you from God,[13] now when you as
a woman, confess and receive Jesus
Christ,[14] you are allowing God to come home
to live in you as He originally planned to
do.[15]

8. DISCOVER that through what Christ suffered on your account, there is nothing left
for you as a woman, to suffer.[16] You are
justified before God.[17] A girl said it like
this: "I am *just-as-if-I'd* never sinned!"

9. DISCOVER that the moment you as a

woman, accept these facts and believe them
and confess Christ as your Lord, you are restored, uplifted, regenerated and reborn to
the God life,[18]   which is what the Bible
calls *salvation.*[19]

1.	Jn.1:12	11.	Re.1:5	16.	Tit.3:5-7
2.	2Co.5:17	12.	Col.1:20-22		Ga.2:16
3.	Ge.1:27		Ro.3:22		Ep.2:8-9
4.	Ge.3		Ps.34:22	17.	Ro.5:1
5.	2Pe.3:9	13.	Ac.10:43	18.	Ac.2:21
6.	Ro.6:23		Mt.26:29		Ac.4:12
7.	Jn.3:16		Is.59:12	19.	1Th.5:9
8.	2Co.5:21		Ro.8:38-39		2Ti.2:10
9.	Ro.8:32-33	14.	Ro.10:9-10		He.5:9
10.	Ep.2:13-16	15.	Ep.2:13		
	Is.53		Ge.3:8		

"The world has enough bigotry and prejudice without getting more from the pulpit or the podium. Christ came to love, to lift, to bless and to save humanity. These are the facts I emphasize to women around the globe."

Chapter 6

DIGNITY FOR WOMEN

KNOWING THAT GOD paid to redeem and to restore womankind to Him, you will no longer condemn or allow others to discredit what God has justified, you will never again treat as second class what He has paid so much to ennoble.

Memorize these six facts about your rich heritage.

1. God is what He says He is.
2. I am what He says I am.
3. God has what He says He has.
4. I have what He says I have.
5. God will do what He says He will do.
6. I can do what He says I can do.

See the You That God Sees

These are the facts I emphasize to women around the globe. Wherever I share them, it lifts people. Multitudes attend our campaigns all over the world. My husband and I proclaim the good news to these masses with gladness and with respect for the divine dignity of each human person — female or male, who is present in our meetings.

The world has enough bigotry and prejudice without getting more from the pulpit or the podium. Christ never came to condemn, to demean or to insult people, but He came to love, to lift, to bless and to save them.[1]

No one has the right to impugn the self-esteem or to abuse the human dignity of a woman by relegating her to an inferior role of ingratiating subservience in the Christian church.

No woman created in God's image needs to bow or to acquiesce to archaic dictums or pronouncements made in the name of God, of the church or of tradition, by someone presuming superiority over women.

Good News — Not Condemnation

Jesus condemned or demeaned no one — not even the adulterous woman and man[2] or the thief on the cross.[3] And as His ambassadors,[4] we do not condemn people.

In Christ there is salvation, dignity and self-esteem for women,[5] not religious servitude or inferiority. In Him there is deliverance[6] and significance for women; not subordination or captivity.

Our message does not wound the sensitive ego of either women or men, but it heals insecurity and inferiority. It nurtures the dignity which God created in humankind. It does not demean one race or color or class or gender as being less competent or significant or valuable than another, but it promotes the divine equality, value, and potential which God created in every person.

We represent Christ. We cannot demean the status or the rank of modern women by imposing upon them social dogmas and patterns of first century cultures. Our message must bring life and joy and peace and divine nobility to every person, on the equal premise of God's redemption.

Christianity is not a set of confining and depressing rules and tenets conscripted from the social orders of the first century. It is the good news that everyone who believes on Christ has been redeemed and restored to God on the same level. Anyone can now rise and walk again with Him.

The most irreligious and unbelieving woman on earth has unlimited possibilities in God. Anyone of any race or of either sex can become a new creature in Christ,[7] and can become His co-worker and representative to this world.

This is your rich heritage. This is the doorway to a new kind of abundant living for every person who reads this book.

A New Beginning

Mark Twain said, "Keep away from people who try to belittle your ambitions. Small people always do that. Great people make you feel that you too, can become great."

The intent of this book is to help you discover that you are vital in God's plan. Destiny is at work in your life. You are God's idea.

Here are eight statements about you as a woman. Rehearse them until they become a part of you.

1.   I am created in God's likeness.
2.   I am unique — one of a kind.
3.   I am of infinite value — to God and to

others.

4.   I am an esteemed daughter in His royal family.
5.   I am loved, in spite of my faults.
6.   I am redeemed and accepted by the Lord.
7.   I am empowered for His divine service to others.
8.   I am commissioned as an ambassador in His royal kingdom.

Remember your rich heritage. Believe what God's word says about you and begin to realize the wonderful lifestyle designed and planned for you as a *Woman Without Limits*.

1.	Jn.3:17	3.	Lu.23:4	6.	Lu.4:18
	Lu.19:10	4.	2Co.5:20	7.	2Co.5:17
2.	Jn.8:11	5.	He.5:9		

PART II

LIBERATED
THROUGH
FORGIVENESS

WITHOUT THE KNOWLEDGE of forgiveness, women search for someone else who can pray for them, because of their own sense of unworthiness. They turn to good works, to philosophy, to "religion", to subservience.

Women who do not know about what Christ has done for them may try church attendance, benevolence, penance, prayers, fastings, confessions, abstention from pleasures and from bad habits, self-denial, pilgrimages, even laceration and punishment of their own bodies, in their insatiable quest for spiritual satisfaction.

But as you read this book, you will discover how every woman has been legally and totally liberated through forgiveness and how she has been made right in God's sight.

The price has already been paid for you as a woman, to have right standing with God and to be His witness, His representative, His ambassador, His messenger to your world.

You are liberated through forgiveness to become all that God has in mind for you to be; to regain your full human dignity and self-esteem, with all of the legal and equal rights of a royal family member — a daughter of God, a true *Woman Without Limits.*

Chapter 7

YOUR WAY TO FREEDOM

REAL FREEDOM IS knowing that nothing in your past can ever cause you guilt, or accuse you, or condemn you, or demean you. This peace and freedom can only be experienced by knowing of and by embracing Christ's redemption.

Some life-changing words were spoken by Jesus to a woman whom the men considered to be of "ill repute." She had an encounter with Jesus. He was the first man who ever esteemed her dignity and her value as a human person.

He said to her, Your sins are forgiven.[1]

Hypocritical pharisees (probably some who themselves had committed adultery) *had asked Jesus to come for lunch.*[2] In some way, this woman heard about the invitation and she *brought an exquisite flask filled with expensive perfume. Going in, she knelt behind Him at His feet, weeping, with her tears falling down upon His feet; she wiped them off with her hair and kissed them and poured the perfume on them.*[3]

Jesus' host said to himself, *"This proves that Jesus is no prophet, for if God had really sent Him, He would know what kind of woman this one is!"*[4] (*This one!* probably indicating that he knew others in his area too.)

Jesus honored the woman's act of respect toward him by responding to His host: *Look! See this woman!* (He recounted what she had done, then said:) *Therefore her sins — and they are many — are forgiven.*[5]

Jesus told the woman whom the unconscious Pharisees smugly characterized as a prostitute: *Your sins are forgiven ... your faith has saved you; go in peace.*[6]

The Miracle of Peace

That word, *peace,* exemplifies the object of Christ's coming. The angels announced at His birth: *Peace on earth, good will toward all people.*[7] Peace is only realized when total forgiveness of all sins is accepted.

The Bible says, *Having been justified by faith, we have peace with God through our Lord Jesus Christ.*[8] *And there is therefore now no condemnation to those who are in Christ Jesus.*[9]

Forgiveness! No Condemnation! Peace! What wonderful words!

Sin brought the penalty of death ... (but) Christ freely takes away sins and gives glorious life instead.[10] That is the object of His coming — to forgive us, to redeem us, to pay for our sins, to justify us, to restore us to God as though we had never sinned.

When sins have been forever forgiven and forgotten, there is no need to offer more sacrifice to get rid of them ... So now we can walk right in ... where God is, because of the blood of Jesus (who has) *opened up for us this fresh, new, life-giving way into the holy presence of God ... with true hearts, fully trusting Him to receive us, because ... Christ's blood makes us clean ...*[11]

1.	Lu.7:48 LB	5.	Lu.7:44-47 LB	9.	Ro.8:1
2.	Lu.7:36 LB	6.	Lu.7:48,50 LB	10.	Ro.5:16 LB
3.	Lu.7:37-38 LB	7.	Lu.2:14	11.	He.10:18-22 LB
4.	Lu.7:39 LB	8.	Ro.5:1		

Daisy believes that her mission
in life is to bring Christ and
His love to people — accessible,
embraceable, tangible.

Chapter 8

WHAT FORGIVENESS MEANS

CHRIST SAYS to you, *I have forgiven your sins!* Those words mean that regardless of your past life, Jesus is saying to you — right now: *Your sins are forgiven!*

All you have to do to experience the peace of Christ is to accept His gift of forgiveness, and to believe in what He has done on your behalf.

To grasp the significance of these ideas and how they affect your personal dignity and self-esteem, understand two things.

First: The background of human suffering and guilt;

Second: The simple, yet profound step God took — out of love and esteem for you, to forgive your sins, to redeem you, to justify you and to restore you to Him. As you study, you will discover how that you as a woman, can be liberated through forgiveness the same as any man can be, and how you have been *made right in God's sight...* so that you can *actually become all that God has had in mind for you to be.*[1]

I write (to tell you), your sins are forgiven you.[2]

Listen! In this man Jesus, there is forgiveness for your sins! Everyone who trusts in Him is freed from all guilt and declared righteous — something (religious) *law could never do.*[3]

The purpose of Christ's coming was to bring God's forgiveness to people. He came to illustrate the lifestyle and the relationship with God which every human person can have.

You only need to believe that *your sins are for-given,* and understand why God has taken legal steps to do this. He blotted out your past so that it can never be held against you.

Jesus is coming to you, to help you to compre-hend the fact that God has forgiven your sins.

Think about these wonderful facts:

* God has forgiven your sins. Therefore, He is not holding anything against you. He is not angry at you.

* God has forgiven your sins. Therefore, He considers you to be His friend. He is not reserv-ing anything to punish you for.

* God has forgiven your sins. You need not be afraid of Him. You no longer need to feel inse-cure before Him. There is only peace between you and God.

* God has forgiven your sins. The day of judgment is no longer a day to dread or to fear. You can never be condemned or convicted of *for-given* sins. You and God are friends. You need never carry a sense of guilt or of fear. There is only peace and tranquility for you. Apprehension

and anxiety are gone.

* God has forgiven your sins. You are truly liberated through forgiveness — liberated *to actually become all that God has had in mind for you to be.*[4]

On what legal grounds has God forgiven your sins, since His word says, *The soul that sins shall die?*[5]

Has God already forgiven your sins — even if you have not asked Him to? Yes, He has. But His gift of forgiveness must be known about and accepted by you in order for you to realize the *peace*[6] and the *glorious life*[7] that comes through being *convinced of the good news that Jesus died for you.*[8]

The Bible contains the *good news that God... makes you right in His sight* — *when you put your faith and trust in Christ.*[9]

True liberation for a woman can only be realized through true forgiveness — through accepting God's forgiveness and through self-forgiveness.

1.	Ro.5:1-2 LB	4.	Ro.5:2 LB	7.	Ro.5:16 LB
2.	1 Jn.2:12	5.	Eze.18:4,20	8.	Col.1:23 LB
3.	Ac.13:38-39 LB	6.	Ro.5:1	9.	Ro.1:17 LB

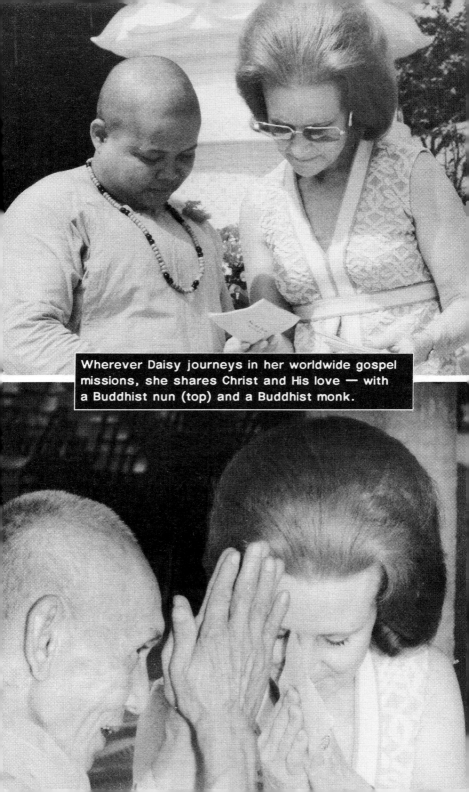

Wherever Daisy journeys in her worldwide gospel missions, she shares Christ and His love — with a Buddhist nun (top) and a Buddhist monk.

Chapter 9

WOMEN NEED FORGIVENESS

LET'S GO BACK to the beginning and see why human persons need God's forgiveness and His new life.

Every individual is created in God's image.[1] Adam and Eve broke God's law, doubted His integrity and disobeyed Him.[2] That was sin, and it resulted in them being separated from God's presence.[3] They forfeited their intimate relationship with God, and became slaves of Satan, their new master whom they chose to believe.

Being the parents of humanity, their sinful nature was engendered in every living person. *All have sinned and come short of the glory of God.*[4]

The Endless Search

Unless a woman has heard about Christ's vicarious death on behalf of every human person, and unless she has accepted His forgiveness and His new life, she is counted as though she is separated from God, because the sinful nature of Adam and Eve is inherent in her.

That is why, without the knowledge of God's forgiveness, you sense guilt and condemnation before Him.

Your sin-consciousness abrogates your faith in God, in the Bible, in others and most of all, in

yourself.   It discourages your initiative.   It breeds
in you an inferiority complex.   You become afraid
of God — even insecure about yourself.

You find no confident approach to your Creator.
You search for someone else who can pray for you
because of your own sense of unworthiness.

This guilt complex of insignificance may cause
you to turn to human philosophy or to religion in
order to suppress your sin-consciousness.

Your search never ends because as a woman,
created in God's likeness, you are made to walk
with Him, to commune and to fellowship with Him,
as Eve did in the garden of Eden.

When sin entered the human race, God's pure
life was forfeited by Eve and Adam alike.

The subconscious search to recover the thing
called "righteousness" (right standing with God) is
the reason for all religions — those of unevange-
lized areas as well as those of the cultured and
philosophical world.

God's Solution

God has made a way for every woman to recover what was lost in the garden of Eden. *He
gives you the power to become His child,*[5] His
daughter, with all of the privileges of being re-born
into His family.

God's word promises: *I will forgive your iniq-
uity, and your sin I will remember no more.*[6]   He
says: *I will bring health and healing ... and you shall*

be to Me ... joy, a praise, and an honor before all ...
who shall hear all the good that I do to you ... and for
all the goodness and all the prosperity that I provide
for you.[7]

God's plan is to cleanse you through giving His
Son, Jesus Christ, to assume all legal punishment
for your sins, so that *He could declare you not*
guilty.[8] That is what I call being liberated through
forgiveness.

1.	Ge.1:27	4.	Ro.3:23; 5:12	7.	Je.33:6,9
2.	Ge.3:1-7	5.	Jn.1:12	8.	Ro.5:9 LB
3.	Ge.3:8,23-24	6.	Je.31:34		

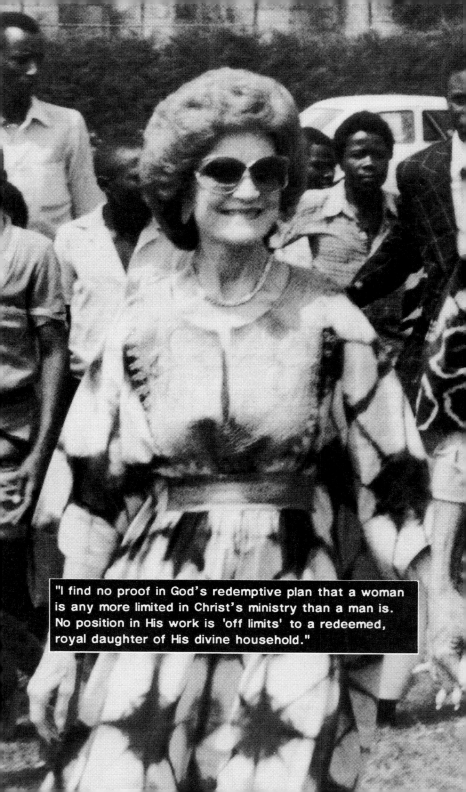

"I find no proof in God's redemptive plan that a woman is any more limited in Christ's ministry than a man is. No position in His work is 'off limits' to a redeemed, royal daughter of His divine household."

Chapter 10

GOD'S GIFT OF FORGIVENESS

IN GOD'S PLAN of forgiveness, *Christ was wounded for your transgressions, He was bruised for your iniquities: the chastisement* (or the punishment which you deserved because of your sin) *was laid upon Him, and by His stripes you were healed* (or, since He endured your punishment, you as a woman, are forgiven — restored to God, and healed of your estrangement from God, with its consequences, if you know about it and believe it.)[1]

Your sins are already judged and punished in Christ. He already assumed your penalty in your place. He did it so that you would be absolved from all guilt, condemnation and judgment.

Since a crime cannot be punished twice, nor can a debt be paid twice, you and I are liberated through forgiveness.

In order to accept God's gift of forgiveness, you need to know about it. *Faith comes by hearing* (or by knowing) *God's word* (God's plan of forgiveness).[2]

Human Efforts

Without the knowledge of this good news, women and men search instinctively to find peace with God through good works, through philosophy, through religion or through other means.

They may try church attendance, benevolence, penance, prayers, fastings, confessions, abstention from pleasures and from bad habits, self-denial, pilgrimages, even laceration and punishment of their own bodies, in their insatiable quest for spiritual satisfaction.

Yet, the tormenting consciousness of sin, of guilt and of unworthiness before God persists as long as you remain uninformed about God's plan of forgiveness and of salvation.*

Christ gave His life to bear the penalty of every sin that you ever committed. You can actually receive God's forgiveness and His righteousness now — just by accepting it in your heart. Then you will be a woman who can stand in God's presence without the sense of fear, of guilt, or of inferiority — just as Eve did before she ever sinned. That is what we call righteousness — or right standing before God.

You are forgiven the moment you accept His love for you. Then you are liberated through that forgiveness.

When you experience that, then *who dares to accuse you? God is the One who has forgiven you and given you right standing with Himself.*[3]

God sent the Good News... that everyone (including every woman) *who believes in Christ will have their sins forgiven through His name.*[4]

---

*My husband, T.L. Osborn, has written a powerful and inspiring book, *The Big Love Plan.* Be sure to get it and read it.

My Message to the World

My ministry, as a woman witness — a woman representative of Jesus Christ, is *to open your eyes, to turn you from darkness to light, from the power of Satan to God, that you may receive the forgiveness of sins.*[5]

The Bible says, *This message of salvation should be taken ... to all nations: There is forgiveness of sins for all who turn to Christ.*[6] We have already taken it to millions of people, face to face, in over 70 nations of the world.

We are now sharing with you the good news that *Jesus Christ... is the One who took* (the punishment of) *your sins upon Himself, and brought you into fellowship with God; and He is the forgiveness of your sins.*[7]

Adam's (and Eve's) sin brought punishment to all, but Christ's righteousness makes you right with God, so you can live.[8]

Sin brought the penalty of death... (but) Christ freely takes away sins and gives glorious life instead.[9]

1.   Is.53:5   4.   Ac.10:42-43 LB   7.   1Jn.2:1-2 LB
2.   Ro.10:17   5.   Ac.26:18   8.   Ro.5:18 LB
3.   Ro.8:33 LB   6.   Lu.24:47 LB   9.   Ro.5:16 LB

This woman was led to an Osborn crusade, blind. Accepting Christ, her sight is restored and she is overjoyed as she counts Daisy's fingers, then watches the audience in wonder as they wave back at her.

Chapter 11

WOMAN'S RESTORATION

THE BIBLE TEACHES that your sins have been put to the account of Jesus, and that He died for their remission, so that His righteousness can be put to your account.[1] That is total forgiveness — total liberation.

The Living Bible says it this way: *For God took the sinless Christ and poured into Him your sins. Then, in exchange, he poured God's goodness into you.*[2]

That happens to you as a woman, the moment you believe on Christ and accept Him — the same as it happens to a man.

You, a woman, have the same right standing with God, and the same right to be His witness, or His representative, or His ambassador, or His messenger. You become a *Woman Without Limits.*

That is good news! God has made the way for your full restoration, so that you have not only re-gained the personal relationship with God that was broken off when sin entered the human race, but your own human dignity, as a woman, is restored.

God has forgiven you and given you right stand-ing with Himself.[3] *He freely takes away sins and gives you His glorious life.*[4]

A Royal Daughter's Rights

That idea may sound too good to be true, but God's good news is that He charged your sins to Christ's account, and then He credited His righteousness to your account.[5] Now, you can stand in His presence with all of the legal and equal rights of a royal family member — a daughter of God[6] a real *Woman Without Limits*.

Right now, you have *salvation through forgiveness of sins.*[7] *Jesus Christ is the One who took your sins upon himself, and brought you into fellowship with God; He is the forgiveness!*[8] *His righteousness makes you right with God, so you can* (really) *live.*[9]

When Jesus suffered the sentence of your sins, you were forever absolved of them.[10] You as a woman, are liberated through forgiveness. As a redeemed and a restored woman, you once again live in God's presence as Eve did in the garden of Eden — a *Woman Without Limits*.

Your Penalty Is Paid

This is the message of the gospel! *This man, Jesus Christ, brought forgiveness ... through God's mercy...*[11] *He gives you right standing with God, which results in eternal life through Jesus Christ your Lord.*[12]

All you need to do is *only believe.*[13]

Your sins can no longer condemn you because Christ put them away forever.[14] You are forgiven!

The full punishment or judgment of all of your

transgressions against God has been suffered.[15] The payment has been made. You are now liberated through forgiveness!

If anyone... rejects the Savior after knowing the truth of forgiveness... there will be nothing to look forward to but... punishment.[16]

But, *happy is the* (woman) *who is declared "not guilty" by God. Blessed are* (the women) *whose sins are forgiven... what joy there is for any* (woman) *whose sins are no longer counted against her by the Lord.*[17]

When God gave His Son and when Jesus gave His life to ransom you from the dominion of sin, that was the proof of how much God loves you and values you as a woman; it is the proof of how much He wants to share His life with you.

* * *

A wonderful new miracle life is beginning in you today. Watch for opportunities to tell others how it has affected you to discover that you have been truly liberated through forgiveness.

1.	2Co.5:21	7.	Lu.1:77 LB	12.	Ro.5:21 LB
2.	2Co.5:21 LB	8.	1Jn.2:2 LB	13.	Mk.9:23
3.	Ro.8:33 LB	9.	Ro.5:18 LB	14.	He.9:26
4.	Ro.5:16 LB	10.	Mt.26:28,	15.	1Pe.2:24
5.	2Co.5:21		He.10:18	16.	He.10:26-27 LB
6.	Jn.1:12	11.	Ro.5:15 LB	17.	Ro.4:6-7 LB

"In Part III, you will learn to uproot four destructive seeds; you will discover four qual-ities for success; and you will conquer five negative attitudes."

PART III

NEW
BEGINNINGS

EVERY STAGE OF LIFE is an open doorway to another re-beginning. Childhood, adolescence, adulthood, married life, parenthood, middle age, maturity, retirement and advanced age all offer dazzling opportunities for growth through new beginnings.

UPROOT these four destructive seeds:

1. The deluding impression that what you see is fact.
2. The despairing impression that failure is final.
3. The restraining impression that change will ruin things.
4. The fatalistic impression that you are the victim of circumstance.

DISCOVER four qualities for achievement:

1. The power of faith to see beyond what is obvious.
2. The courage to know that you are never defeated unless you give up.
3. The knowledge that you are in absolute control of your reaction to any circumstance.
4. The adventure of growing through change as you welcome the experience of new beginnings.

Every *Woman Without Limits* learns to conquer these five negative attitudes:

1. The selfishness that shrinks her.
2. The prejudice that blinds her.
3. The indifference that isolates her.
4. The envy that erodes her.
5. The greed that consumes her.

To re-begin is to adventure — to grow. Life is a process of changes and of new beginnings. Nothing stays the same.

To win in life, choose to welcome change. To resist change is to lose. You can choose to re-begin and to become a total *Woman Without Limits.*

Chapter 12

BECOMING A NEW WOMAN

WHEN YOU ARE born again, you as a woman, begin to live again.

When you are redeemed and restored to God, you are ready for a new start because you have His new nature within you.

The Living Bible says, *You become a brand-new person inside*[1] — a brand new woman.

The King New James version of that verse says that *you are a new creation; old things have passed away; all things have become new.*[2]

Jesus the Re-Beginner

Each new discovery about Jesus Christ is like another new birth and it inevitably brings change. Change invites more changes and more readjustments, all of which spell g-r-o-w-t-h, or new beginnings.

Believe that you can re-begin.

When Luke wrote his brief summary of Christ's ministry on earth, he referred to *all that Jesus BEGAN to do and teach.*[3] Jesus came to re-begin things, because the old system of religious laws, rules and rituals had not succeeded in restoring people to God.

Through all of the complexities of the law with its judgments and Judaic religious traditions, the chasm between God and people could never be spanned through the offering up of animal sacrifices, as the Old Testament prescribed.

God, who created us wanted us near Him as His friends and partners. He sent Jesus to bring us a new beginning.

Jesus brought to us new knowledge about God — that He is good, that He is not angry with us. He demonstrated that God values every human person — women the same as men, in His plan. He confirmed that God needs us now as His representatives, to be His flesh in action, to be His touchableness, His tangibleness, His reflection on earth.

Jesus opened the way for you and for me to re-begin again and again — as often as we need to in order to know true fulfillment in life.

Decide today that, regardless of your past, or your failures, or your frustrations, you can experience a new beginning that will lead you into the blessed lifestyle which God planned for you as a *Woman Without Limits*. Decide to believe that you can re-begin.

The only way abortions and divorces or miscarriages and misfortunes of the past can encumber your path or limit your future, is if you choose to allow them to.

1.   2 Co.5:17 LB
2.   2 Co.5:17 NJK
3.   Ac.1:1

Chapter 13

CHOOSING TO RE–BEGIN

YOU CANNOT CONTROL the things which come your way but you can control how you react to them. You can choose the thoughts which you think and the actions which you initiate.

You have the God-given ability in you to be self-controlled, and to maintain self-respect and self-value regardless of what others say or do to affect your life.

Situations and circumstances are principally what you think they are. The only things that really affect your life are the things which take shape within your own thinking.

Unhappiness or discouragement is a choice — a choice of the thoughts which you decide to entertain.

Excitement and enthusiasm for life spring from a choice of thoughts.

The Adventure of Change

We can always re-begin by taking command of our own attitude, by learning whatever valuable lesson we can from our past experiences, and by projecting their benefits into a re-beginning of life to be all that God designed us to be.

Re-beginnings involve and produce changes.

T.L. AND DAISY OSBORN CRUSADES

AFRICA

S. AMERICA

INDONESIA

CARIBBEAN

PHILIPPINES

Human tendency is toward tradition. Most people follow beaten paths. They find security in what is conventional or ordinary or commonplace.

Adjustments and fear of the unknown frighten most people, causing them to resist, to rebuff or to reject new beginnings.

To re-begin is to adventure — to grow. Life is a process of changes and of new beginnings. Nothing stays the same. Everything and everyone is constantly changing.

Every stage of life is an open doorway to another re-beginning. Childhood, adolescence, adulthood, married life, parenthood, middle age, maturity, retirement and advanced age all offer dazzling opportunities for growth through new beginnings.

I wish every child could be seeded with a love for the adventure of life so that every change or adjustment or surprise — positive or negative — would be welcomed as a growing experience in life.

The process of change and of growth never ends. Yet for many people, these adjustments precipitate endless traumatic reactions and keep them in turmoil and in confusion.

To be inflexible and to resist changes produces a kind of sterility in life and it causes great unhappiness, conflict and distress.

Chapter 14

MEETING CHANGE WITH COURAGE

I KNOW OF A LADY who faced a most shocking disaster, but who coped and made a new life of service to people.

Helen (as I shall call her) had been a reporter, living a dynamic life surrounded by theatrical and political people, with celebrities as her friends. Then deformative arthritis and diabetes devastated her lifestyle.

Rather than to brood and to lament her loss of mobility and her near blindness, she calculated her possibilities. She could use her eyes — for an hour at a time, she could talk and she could type — with one hand.

She coped with drastic changes, but she did it with positiveness and with self-dignity, grasping each opportunity to transform her problems into possibilities.

She found a new environment, plunged into a new community and began writing children's books. She successfully created a new lifestyle, and literally re-began. She believed that God's purpose for her life was to be of service to people and to help to make them better and happier.

Before long, the new community recognized her

value.   Friends and neighbors sought her out for
counsel and for inspiration.   Children across the
nation fell in love with her books that built character and self-value.

Helen met her disaster with courage.   She
gained through the pain of her readjustments.   She
believed that she could re-begin.   She took control
of her situation and forged it into something beautiful and productive for God and for people.

Self-Esteem for the Tough Team

A husband-wife doctor team arrived in America
as refugees, unable to speak English and unable to
practice medicine.

How easy it would have been for them to exist
on welfare.   They could have wasted their energies
in self-pity over the calamitous events which devastated their professional lives.   But they chose to
believe that they could re-begin.

They belong to God's success club.

They began to study English, and after long
months of hard work, were able to retake the
necessary medical examinations so that they could
qualify as licensed physicians.

Day after day, instead of bewailing their disad-
vantages and their misfortunes, they chose to think
about their abilities and their opportunities for new
beginnings.

To maintain an existence during their re-educa-
tion, they found jobs as domestic servants and saved

enough to open a small candy store that flourished.

Finally they received their licenses to practice medicine. They went to a rural area where the people lacked adequate medical service, and soon became recognized throughout that farm community. Their practice became very successful.

They were able to give back some of what God had given to them through the American dream of freedom for new beginnings.

Transcending Depression

That husband-wife team was forced by circumstances to die or to re-begin. Working as domestic servants, they kept their self-dignity and lived with pride.

When negative, self-demeaning thoughts dominate your mind, you are dying while your body is still living. You are the only one who can exercise the power of choice to erase those depressive attitudes and to stand up tall and look beyond the bleak barriers that conspire to destroy or to restrain you. You have the power to reappraise events, to perceive new possibilities, and to grow through new beginnings.

Nothing can stop you from fulfillment in life when you believe in the power to re-begin.

Daisy addresses thousands of women, besides men and children, at her National Women's Miracle Day during one of the crusades abroad.

Chapter 15

FROM DESTRUCTION TO PRODUCTION

ONE OF THE GREATEST experiences I have ever had was coping with the despair and the tragedy of the Ugandan people when I went there to prepare for that enormous Kampala crusade. The crowds numbered over a quarter of a million people, day after day.

The light of hope had been extinguished in the hearts of the citizens. Their lives and their nation had been demoralized through fourteen years of civil war and deterioration.

Practically every family had sustained heartache, destruction, brutality, rape, murder, robbery, pillage and havoc. They had become hostages of despair and hopelessness.

God impressed us one day that it was time to go into Uganda to organize a great national gospel crusade to restore hope and faith to this nation of people that had been abandoned to despair.

We knew that He had sent His angel ahead of us, and that we would find favor with the government and with the people.

The Lord showed us that He was sending us to tell those disheartened people that they could rise and become productive again if they could believe in the power to re-begin with Christ.

After I had spent almost six weeks organizing, preaching, ministering, meeting with committees and doing all within my power to cover the areas of the nation that were not in war, my husband joined me from the USA, and the crusade opened with a great multitude of people.

Day after day I, or my husband, would stretch out our arms to that mass of hurting humanity and tell them how God had sent us to speak these things to them in His name:

"Uganda, I love you. Uganda, I have not forsaken you. Uganda, I need you. Uganda, do not despair. If you will look to me and call on me, I will save you. I will heal you. I will help you. I will give you a new beginning. I will give you a new future!"

Re-Birthed for Re-Beginning

Hope and faith were re-born in the heart of that nation. Despair was transcended by a new birth of courage, of confidence, and of a new awareness of Jesus Christ as their friend and partner in life.

In meeting after meeting, we told the people:

"Whatever your plight, look beyond it — and look with pride and with faith in your hearts, because God is unveiling a brand-new tomorrow for Uganda.

"You have received His message and believed in

His love.   You have accepted the good news that God has not forsaken you.   You are marching into a new future."

We would often say:

"You may be dressed in tattered clothes or lack shoes for your feet. But with Christ in your life, walk with pride because you are being re-birthed into a re-beginning with God.

"In the near future you will again be dressed to befit the distinguished people of this Pearl of Africa. Your businesses and your crops will flourish again."

Since that prophetic crusade, those new beginnings have taken place and the nation has been re-birthed with pride and with new faith in their future.

Forgiving Your Past
Focusing Your Future

One day, as I preached to that field of Ugandans, the Spirit of the Lord impressed me to command the evil spirits of hatred and of malice to leave the people.

A precious woman, Betty Andiru, was brought there by friends who had to restrain her from harming anyone. She was barking like a wild dog. She had mentally collapsed due to repeated rapings and beatings by roving soldiers who had captured her as their slave.*

She hated those men and constantly plotted her revenge. But finally she broke, as repeated brutalities drove her insane.

As I preached about Christ's power to re-begin, the presence of Jesus Christ changed Betty. The demons of hatred left her and she was inundated by a baptism of love for everyone — including those who had tortured her.

She wept as she witnessed to the multitude telling them: "Now I am well. The demons that possessed me because of my hatred, have gone. I love everyone now. I have done what you have said. Jesus has forgiven my past and He has given to me a new beginning."

---

*Get our 554 page Classic Documentary, *The Gospel According to T.L. and Daisy*. The accounts of this and many other notable miracles will be a life-long inspiration in your life.

Chapter 16

GOD BELIEVES IN YOU

MY HUSBAND WROTE four powerful lines about people whose lives have been injured or brutalized or disgraced or who have made careless or destructive mistakes. He did it to express Christ's attitude toward them and to encourage them to believe that they can re-begin. His lines:

> Regardless of your past,
> I still believe in you.
> Remember! You're not trash,
> I've come to live in you.

When Jesus Christ enters a life, He comes to initiate new beginnings. He brings a new birth of self-worth.

Serving God — Serving People

In the twenty-fifth chapter of Matthew, Jesus commended those who feed the hungry, who clothe the naked, who give drink to the thirsty and who visit the sick and the prisoners.

Those who do these deeds of kindness are totally unaware that they are doing those things to Jesus.

They are simply doing what comes natural to a believer — helping, lifting, blessing and loving people who are hurting and who are in need.

T.L. and Daisy dedicated their lives, when they were married to obey Christ and to preach His gospel to all the world. Below: They had been to India and had failed, because they did not understand the real living power of the gospel. As young pastors in the state of Oregon, the Lord met them in some extra-ordinary experiences. They both re-committed their lives to share Christ with the whole world.

"He never left Himself without a witness; there were always His reminders." Ac. 14:17 LB "I will do for you the wonderful thing I have promised." Ac. 13:34 LB

DAISY AND HER HUSBAND, T.L. OSBORN

Jesus said: "You did not choose Me, but I chose you, and appointed you that you should go and bear fruit, and that your fruit should remain, that whatever you ask the Father in My name, He may give you." Jn. 15:16

Christ's words will be a total surprise when He says: *Inasmuch as you did it to one of the least of these, you did it to Me.*[1]

The only way we can express our love for God is by expressing His love to people. The only way we can serve God is by serving people.

Every time you reach out to a human person who is in need or who is hurting or who is in distress or in despair, you are reaching out to serve Jesus Christ.

Every time you choose to do that, you choose the miraculous re-birth of hope and of courage that brings fresh music, new laughter, a new song and new fulfillment to your life.

Music From the Basement

An elderly street-person asked if he could spend a cold winter night in the cluttered basement of an apartment house in Europe.

After a few hours, the owner of the house heard music from the basement, and she found the man playing on an old discarded harp.

She asked: "How did you repair my harp? No one else could do it."

The old gentleman replied: "When I was young, I made this very harp, and when you make something, you can repair it!"

Christ who gave His life to give you a new birth is the One who can help you to re-begin.

1.   Mt.25:40

Chapter 17

A BRAND NEW WOMAN

THE BIBLE SPEAKS of *living a brand-new kind of life that is continually learning more and more of what is right, and being more and more like Christ.*[1]

Four Impressions — Four Qualities

There are four impressions to keep in focus, as a *Woman Without Limits:*

1. The deluding impression that what you see is fact.

2. The despairing impression that failure is final.

3. The restraining impression that change will ruin things.

4. The fatalistic impression that you are the victim of circumstances.

There are four vital qualities which guarantee success in your new beginnings as a *Woman Without Limits:*

1. The power of faith to see beyond what is obvious.

2. The courage to know that you are never defeated unless you give up.

3.   The knowledge that you are in absolute control of your reaction to any circumstance.

4.   The adventure of growing through change as you welcome the experiences of new beginnings.

To never re-begin is to never hope again. To abandon hope is to say "I don't believe in God." It is to say, "I don't care about life — not mine, not yours, not anybody's."

Human persons all around us are lonely and hurting, forsaken and unloved. You and I can team up with Jesus Christ and actually be a part of bringing His blessings to them, by lifting burdens, by healing hurts, by consoling sorrows and by solving problems. Every time we do that, we extend to somebody else the gift of a new beginning. That is what Christ extended to us when He saved us. Now, that is what we can do, in His name, for others.

Learning for Winning

Erich Fromm says: "Not the one who has much is rich, but the one who gives much. Whoever is capable of giving of themselves is rich."

We re-begin to feed the hungry, and we are fed. We visit the sick and those in prison, and we re-discover Christ. We clothe the naked, and we find ourselves dressed in newness. We give water to the thirsty and we discover a new fountain of life.

As we give, we receive. As we lift, we are raised.

As we welcome the adventure of change and as we perceive the potential of new beginnings, we discover the process and the delight of living life on a greater scale than we ever dreamed of before.

Refuse and reject any and every kind of religious or secular fatalism that denies you the freedom to choose your way and to strike out in new directions.

Jesus said to *repent and believe the gospel.*[2]

Repentance means the opportunity of a new start, the chance to gain by past pain, and to project new knowledge with new ideas, new visions and new hopes, into a new tomorrow and to begin again.

Every *Woman Without Limits* learns to conquer these five negative attitudes:

* The selfishness that shrinks her.
* The prejudice that blinds her.
* The indifference that isolates her.
* The envy that erodes her.
* The greed that consumes her.

You become an achiever in life when you discover the power of new beginnings and the fact that there are no limits for the woman who identifies with Christ.

1.   Col.3:10 LB
2.   Mk.1:15

"You become an achiever in life when you discover the fact that there are no limits for the woman who identifies with Christ in His mission of love to a hurting world of people."

PART IV

FROM
TRADITION
TO
FREEDOM

JESUS INTRODUCED new values, new possibilities and new opportunities for women. He contravened religious dogmas in order to unfetter womankind from the demeaning restraints of antiquated religious and cultural rules.

He lifts people from tradition to freedom. By His action, He is saying, "Woman, you are released! You are forgiven! You are redeemed! You are justified! You are restored to God! You are valued! You are needed! You can be my witness, my messenger, my representative, my ambassador, my spokesperson!"

Always remember: Your designated place is to follow Jesus and the submission that you need to be concerned about is your submission to Him. This is God's good news for you. He paid a big price to buy your freedom.

Resolve to no longer be restrained by the shackles of outdated religious bigotry and discrimination. Practice the daily awareness of your freedom in Jesus Christ.

Stand up! Respond to Christ's call to dignity and to destiny in His plan. No position in His work is "off limits" to you as a redeemed, royal daughter in His divine household.

Chapter 18

WOMAN, YOU ARE FREE!

THERE IS A STORY in the gospel of Luke that is timeless in its message. In fact, each account we have of Christ's encounters with people contains an up-to-date message for us today.

Jesus displayed the nature, the love and the will of our heavenly Father in everything that He did.[1] We can trust His example, and we are to emulate His attitude and His conduct in every relationship that we have with people. That is the way we strive for perfection in Christ.[2]

God's Character Comes Through

When Jesus walked the delicate religious "tightrope", teaching in the synagogues and addressing religious people, God's character of love was always evidenced.

The Bible says: Jesus was teaching in one of the synagogues on the Sabbath. There was a seriously handicapped woman who had been bent double for eighteen years and was unable to straighten herself.[3]

When Jesus saw her, He called her to Him and said, "Woman, you are loosed from your infirmity."[4]

And He laid His hands on her, and immediately she was made straight, and glorified God.[5]

Following this demonstration of God's gentle
love for a dear lady, the Bible relates a typical
demonstration of religious contempt.

The synagogue ruler answered with indignation,
because Jesus had healed on the Sabbath; and he said
to the crowd, "There are six days in which to work;
in them, come and be healed, and not on the Sabbath
day."[6]

Christ's response: *"Hypocrite! Does not each*
one of you on the Sabbath loose his ox or his donkey
from the stall, and lead it away to water it?

"So ought not this woman, being a daughter of
Abraham, whom Satan has bound — think of it — for
eighteen years, be loosed from this bond on the
Sabbath."[7]

Sounds of Liberation

For nearly 2,000 years those words of Jesus
have endured. *"Woman, you are loosed"* — Woman,
you are free!

Today, women around the world are responding
to those liberating words of Christ. They are
standing up and they are embracing the fact that
God's plan of redemption frees them from inferiority, from ignominy, from second class citizenry,
from insignificance and from other cultural and religious discriminations which limit or obstruct them
for public ministry in Christ's service.

I like the way Jesus spoke to that woman in
the synagogue. He addressed her using the only
non-prejudicial title by which she could be called:

Woman — not wife, mother, sister or daughter, any of which titles would have categorized her as being the property of some man — her husband, her brother, her father, her owner.

Jesus addressed her as *Woman.* It was the one title which respected her individual human worth, her own dignity, her unique value as a human person created in God's image. *Woman* — the female expression of God.

Had Christ addressed her by any other title, an immediate classification would have been made, and a cultural value established. A widow had a certain value, a wife another, a mother of a son yet another, and of course a virgin daughter had an exclusive rating.

Regardless of your social status, your identity as a woman distinguishes you as God's creation, fashioned in His own image.[8]   Indeed, you are God's idea. It is very important to remember your worth. The same price was paid to redeem you as was paid for everyone else.[9] No one is inferior. Every person is equally endowed with excellence, created in God's class of being.

Never permit religious leaders or rulers to intimidate you or to denigrate you or to diminish your own self-value as a woman. Jesus never demeaned or disparaged anyone, but He was always careful to extend respect and esteem to each one whom He addressed, without regard for their social status, their race or their gender.

Jesus Christ is the same yesterday, and today and forever.[10] He sees you where you are, as you are.   If you are being handicapped or muzzled or bridled by religious restraints, He is ready to release you.   Trust Him and He will lift you from tradition to freedom.

1.	Jn.5:19;	4.	Lu.13:12	8.	Ge.1:27
	Jn.14:9	5.	Lu.13:13 NKJ,LB,RV,NIV	9.	Jn.3:16-17
2.	Mt.5:48	6.	Lu.13:14	10.	He.13:8
3.	Lu.13:10-11 LB	7.	Lu.13:15-16		

Chapter 19

RELIGIOUS CONCEIT CONFRONTED

WHEN JESUS GAVE that impaired woman in the synagogue her freedom, the ruler reacted with indignation.

This religious superior was so intent on following the letter of their law that he missed the greatest opportunity of his life. God in the flesh had visited his synagogue, but he never recognized Him. His religious bigotry completely blinded his mind.

Jesus called him a hypocrite. He was saying: "You pretend to represent God but inside you are a cruel, insensitive person. You were entrusted with the laws of God, but you have perverted them in order to guard your traditions. You have segregated and discriminated against people in order to validate your own prejudice."

Religion — An Attitudinizer

Religion is often a sanctimonious system without God's love at its center. When that is the case, it paints a distorted picture of God. This ruler did not recognize God in the flesh because his concept of Him was that He is harsh, uncaring, judgmental, restrictive and insensitive.

Embracing ecclesiastical religion without the

compassion of Jesus Christ, can make people oblivious to the needs of hurting humanity. Laws can become more vital than lives. Rules and rituals can become more valued than people.

Religion has been called an opiate which can anesthetize people, making them insensitive to the real needs of others. It can pervert human emotions into the cruel lethargy of inaction.

Religion is an attitudinizer. Religious indoctrinators such as this ruler of the synagogue where Jesus was teaching, distort people's attitudes toward God and toward each other.

Guard your attitude by examining the seeds sown in your mind. Check them against the life and teachings of Jesus. Repel the false seeds; be receptive to the seeds of truth.

That stooped woman to whom Jesus called attention that day in the synagogue, exemplified human need as it stands ...

> Between religion and relation;
> Between law and love;
> Between tradition and truth;
> Between contempt and compassion;
> Between disgrace and God's grace.

Chapter 20

BELIEF BASED ON BIAS

DISCRIMINATION WAS UNYIELDING in both the Jewish temples and in their synagogues. Their seating arrangement, their ceremonies and their teachings emphasized the distinction between people and God, between Jews and Gentiles, between men and women, and between priests and people.

The temple building, including the foyer, was divided into six separate areas or courts, rising one above another.*

The Court of the Gentiles was the only part to which foreigners were admitted. This court was also located on the lowest level and was outside the actual temple.

The Sacred Enclosure was above the Gentile Court, and non-Jews were forbidden to pass beyond their segregated area, under penalty of death.

The Court of Women was higher than the Sacred Enclosure. There Jewish women were permitted to enter, but were strictly forbidden to go beyond it.

The Court of Israel rose above the Court of Women. Only male Jews were permitted to enter.

The Court of Priests was yet three feet above the Court of Israel, and it was reserved for the priests.

----

*Thompson Chain Reference Bible, Study item 4319.

The House of God, eight feet above the Court of the Priests, was divided into two compartments, The Holy Place and The Holy of Holies. Priests entered into the Holy Place to perform certain duties at specific times, but only the high priest could enter the Holy of Holies, once a year, on the Day of Atonement.

Imposed Religious Isolation

Jewish synagogues were patterned after their temples and the segregation of women from the worship area was strictly enforced. They were confined to a separate gallery, or behind lattice where their presence would not be a distraction.

Discriminating barriers faced that woman who was bent when she came to the synagogue that day.

I believe that Jesus knew that needy woman was coming. He also knows about you. As you are reading this good news, Jesus is ready to make contact with you. Be sensitive to His voice.

Tradition or Truth?

Religion does interesting things to people. In over 70 nations I have observed the product of most of the religions of the world. I have decided that the culture of a nation, her traditions, her customs and her attitudes are molded by her religions.

I have seen the twins which Religion births — Culture and Tradition. They make slaves and menial servants out of women. Religious devotees go through life doing what they are expected to do rather than what they choose to do. They live with obligations rather than options. They bow to rules and requirements instead of enjoying the pleasure of responding to and of cultivating God's ability within them.

Always remember: Follow Jesus. The submission that you need to be concerned about is your submission to Him. This is God's good news for you. He paid a big price to buy your freedom.

Christ has made us free. Now make sure that you stay free and don't get all tied up again in the chains of slavery to Jewish laws and ceremonies.[1] That was Paul's advice to both women and to men.

The Amplified Bible says it like this: *In* (this) *freedom Christ has made us free — completely liberated us; stand fast then, and do not be hampered and held ensnared and submit again to a yoke of slavery — which you have once put off.*

Limited, Labeled but Learning

This gravely handicapped woman put forth the effort necessary to get to that synagogue. And what Jesus did to her that day had never been done by a rabbi.

As Christ was teaching, I can imagine Him, looking around, with a keen sensitivity and a sharp alertness to the needs of His listeners. He saw the ruler of the synagogue. He observed some important Jewish men in their special seats of honor. He pondered the sanctuary full of patriarchal Jews.

But He kept looking, His discerning eyes pen-

etrating the barrier which obstructed the women
from view.   His attention centers on that lame,
limited and labeled woman of low esteem.

Hallmarking Womankind

As Jesus looked beyond and above those pre-
sumptuous, prejudiced men, fresh hope and faith
were born in the women's gallery that day.   Every
eye was on Him.   God was going into action.   It
was time for a condemnation of divisions, and for
a proclamation of priorities.   It was time for the
hallmarking of womankind and the denouncement of
discrimination.

Jesus called the woman forward[2] — up to the
place where He was speaking.

In that invitation, that woman perceived the kind
of love and compassion that gave her the strength
and courage needed to obey Christ's call.   Despite
the self-impugning violation of Jewish tradition
which her response would imply, she trusted Jesus
more than she feared the religious ruler.   Though
forbidden by tradition to enter the court where
Christ was speaking, she responded to His invitation and acted on His words.

It takes courage to be what Jesus wants you to
be.   You can be a *Woman Without Limits* only if
you do not fear what people think about you.   The
early believers said, *We ought to obey God rather
than men.*[3]

As a woman, resolve to never embrace the
submissive, silent, inferior roles which have been
cast for you.   When you respond to Jesus as Lord

of your life, you have no other master.   Jesus desires to express His love and His leadership
through you.   Never oblige Him to be limited or
shackled by the restraints of ancient religious rules
for women of other epochs.   Remember you are a
Woman Without Limits.

The Christian woman believer who bows to
cultural restrictions and to religious restraints more
than she does to Christ's words, is limiting Jesus
who craves expression through her.   *Your body is
the temple of the Holy Spirit.*[4]   The Holy Spirit in
you is not meant to be silent or to be circumscribed
by restraints.

Jesus called the woman who was bent over, to
Himself.   He was not ashamed to identify with her
in public.   And He is not ashamed of you.   He
identifies with you — as you are, where you are.
His attitude toward this woman shows God's character and His nature toward you.

Jesus has never changed.   He transformed re-
striction to restoration, isolation to realization,
degradation to jubilation, resignation to decision,
bondage to freedom, and chains to change.   *And
Jesus Christ is the same yesterday, and today, and
forever.*[5]

1.   Ga.5:1 LB   4.   1Co.6:19
2.   Lu.13:12 NIV   5.   He.13:8
3.   Ac.5:29

Carida had been bedfast for four months, unable to stand or to walk. Carried to an Osborn Crusade, she received Christ and was healed as Daisy proclaimed the liberating facts of Christ's redemption. Now she weeps with joy, as she shows the crowd what the Lord has done for her.

Chapter 21

INVALIDATING RULES
THAT INCRIMINATE WOMEN

CHRIST'S ACTION that day in the synagogue resolutely invalidated five strict religious laws in order to prioritize a human person — a woman.

What He did illustrated that you need never bow or submit to outdated ecclesiastical ordinances or to patriarchal dogmas and rules which demean your personhood or which discredit your individual value as a human being created in God's image.

Discover your own dignity and your own destiny as God's friend, as His partner and as His representative on earth — a *Woman Without Limits*.

Courageous and Cured

Reading about that woman in Luke, chapter 13, alerts me to the hurting human needs of women around the world. Millions of them are not only stooped or limited physically but they are bowed and they are crouched in their mental attitudes toward life; they are bent in their spirits by the unbearable weight and the unfair burden of religious rules and of discriminating doctrines regarding women.

The mother of Kariuki, the notorious madman who was delivered from demons in one of our East African crusades, was a vivid example. From early childhood she had been obliged to carry loads

of wood — like only an animal should need to bear
— far beyond her physical capacity.   As a result,
her spine was damaged and she was bent double and
could not lift herself up.   After her son was
miraculously restored to sanity, Kariuki's mother
decided to put forth the effort to attend our mass
crusade.

For the first time in her life, that dear Kikuyu
tribeswoman heard the good news of Jesus and she
accepted Him as her personal savior.   She was instantly freed from her bondage.   She could stand
up, bend, jump, run and she was completely healed.
She was a totally freed woman.

Jesus is still calling women who are bent under
impossible burdens, to come to Him for His blessing.   He cares about you.   He desires to lift your
burdens and to give you the strength to stand up, to
be free from your psychological, physical and spiritual bondage.   Then He wants to minister to the
needs of other hurting people, and to lift them
through you.

Identified, Dignified and Justified

It required a great deal of courage for this
bent woman in the Bible to breach the part of the
synagogue where Jesus was speaking.   She had to
violate dogmatic religious traditions in order to respond to Christ's call.   That is what you and I as
women, must often do in order to obey our Lord.

When Jesus called out to the woman, she left
the segregated gallery, descended the stairs, and
crossed the sacred threshold of the men's area.
Every head was turned in her direction.   Every eye

was fixed either on Jesus, or on the woman who was the object of His compassionate attention.

She risked being condemned by religious purists, or even being stoned later for violating a sacred area of the synagogue where only men were allowed to enter.

Jesus was also at risk in what He did. Jewish law prescribed a stiff penalty for anybody who desecrated venerable synagogue rules, or who violated the Sabbath, or for doing work on the holy day.[1] Healing was looked on as being work.

As the woman who was bent double braced herself on her knees for support, she slowly moved toward the speaker. Jesus could have met her at the entryway, to avoid humiliation or reprisal. But the Bible says that *He called her to Him.*[2]

Jesus deliberately repudiated their discrimination against women and called her into the sacred worship area for male Jews where He was speaking. This action was a dramatic illustration of Christ's liberation of women from gender restraints.

As the woman breached the area of worship that was off limits to her, Jesus reassured her saying, *Woman, you are loosed from your infirmity.*[3]

Then as she came near, *Jesus laid His hands on her.*[4] Why did He do that? He had already spoken and His words had brought healing. Was that not sufficient? Why did He make physical contact with her, which was a highly offensive vi-

olation of their religious culture, and why did He
do it publicly?

Five Religious Rules

It is wonderful to see the nature of our heavenly Father at work in His Son, Jesus that day.
For countless centuries, religious tradition and culture had demeaned women, classifying them as inferior, incompetent and insignificant.   Women were
sentenced by both civic laws and by societal standards to a perennial status of servitude and to ignominy.

Now Jesus was invalidating those demoralizing
traditions concerning womankind.   In this one encounter, He contradicted at least five religious
rules:

FIRST: He spoke to the woman in public, an
act forbidden in His culture.

SECOND: He brought her into the area of the
synagogue which was reserved for men — an in-
fringement of the sacred domain which was limited
to Jewish males;

THIRD: He brought her to the speaker's area
— a distinct desecration of a very sacred part of
the synagogue;

FOURTH: He publicly healed the woman on
the Sabbath day, which was considered work — a
punishable violation of the holy day.

Now He would commit a FIFTH offense: He
touched the woman in public — a serious breach of

religious law and of cultural restraints.

Here were five violations of religious law that became five steps of grace for that woman.

She cooperated. She was obedient. She was courageous. She cast religious rules and regulations aside and accepted Jesus as being greater than tradition or culture. And because she was obedient, she was made whole.

Change Your World

You are no different. Decide to obey your Lord Jesus in spite of traditions or rules which are contrived to curtail or to restrain you. When you do, you will experience a new completeness, psychologically, physically and spiritually. Release your religious hang-ups. They will never lead you to God.

1.   Ex.31:14;   3.   Lu.13:12
      Nu.15:32-35   4.   Lu.13:13
2.   Lu.13:12

Daisy proclaims the gospel at Municipal Stadium in Surabaya, Java, (Below) Osborn daughter, LaDonna, pastor of International Gospel Center at Tulsa, OK, preaches Christ at stadium in Papua New Guinea.

Chapter 22

FREEDOM FOR WOMEN

JESUS SAID to the physically stooped lady in Luke, chapter 13, *Woman, be free!* What a command! What a declaration! What an opportunity! When Jesus says you can be free, embrace the fact that He lifts you from tradition to freedom, that He wills for you to be a *Woman Without Limits*.

You are set at liberty from the dominion of Satan. Sin no longer has power over you. You no longer need to submit to the control of any person or system that restricts your God-given abilities.

You are unchained from religious traditional restrictions. You are able to untangle and overcome your psychological problems. You are valuable. Jesus esteems you. You are important to His dream for humankind. He needs you to minister His love to people. God wills to show His magnificent mercy through you. Do not remain bowed in subservience. Respond to the call of your redeemer, Jesus Christ.

Be as courageous in your approach to Jesus as that impaired woman was in Bible days. For eighteen years she had been unable to stand upright.

How many Sabbaths had come and gone for her, without ever receiving encouragement, or healing, or consolation or help? How many painful journeys had she made to the synagogue? But the day Jesus met her there, her world was changed.

And He will change you and your world too.

Woman, you are loosed from your infirmity.[1]
You are released!   You are forgiven!   You are par-
doned!   You are redeemed!   You are liberated!   You
are justified!   You are restored to God!   You are
lifted from tradition to freedom!   Those are
Christ's words to you.

Jesus made that pronouncement about womankind for time and for eternity.   He says those
words to you.   *Woman, you are loosed!*   You are
valued.   You can be my witness.   You can preach.
You can teach.   You can be My messenger, My
ambassador, My representative!   The patriarchy
may not esteem you, but I do.   Male theologians
may forbid you from public ministry, but I have redeemed you and I have chosen you to *be witnesses
unto Me ... to the end of the earth*[2] (anywhere and to
anyone).

Be courageous and cooperate with your Lord.
He is calling you to Him.   He is telling you:
Woman, you are loosed from your infirmity.   Your
bond is broken.   Your chains are dissolved.   You
are unrestrained, unlimited, unshackled.   He is
saying to you, "You are my co-worker now."

Prioritizing Humankind

You may not be like that woman in the Bible
was: Bent in a demeaning position, physically,
looking at feet while others were able to lift themselves to see the sunshine and the blue sky.   She
had been gazing at impossibilities while others could
see opportunities.   She had been restricted and limited while others were disencumbered and free.

But you may be bending under the demeaning yoke of incrimination because of your gender. The burden of being restrained and repressed in your restricted roles of ministry may be causing you to bow and to acquiesce in your attitude about yourself — and about women in general.

Jesus gave that woman power to stand up, to step up, to look up and to rise up to a status she had never known before. She faced new possibilities that day because she had the courage and the confidence to respond to His call.

The Bible says, *When the Son makes you free, you are indeed free.*[3] *You shall know the truth and the truth shall make you free.*[4]

Jesus did not submit to the religious system. He contravened it any time the dignity or the value of a human person was demeaned or depreciated. He brought a new day to humanity. He introduced new values and new thinking. He ushered in new possibilities and new opportunities.

Jesus took His message not only to the open public where women, as well as men, could listen; He also took it to the center of religion, to the platform of male orthodoxy, where He reflected God's attitude toward all human persons on an equal basis.

No other teacher had stood in the synagogue and resolutely invalidated those five strict religious rules in order to prioritize a human person — a woman.

When Jesus contradicted religious dogma in order to unfetter that disabled woman, He did it for you as well as for her. He showed how unconventional God is, how available He is to any human person in need, and how no ordinance of religion can alter, regiment or circumscribe God.

God is love! He has always been and will always be love. If your religion teaches otherwise, Jesus says to you, *Woman, be loosed from your infirmity!* Walk out of your bondage. March toward Jesus Christ like that woman did. Embrace the fact that no position and no place in God's work is off limits to you as a redeemed woman.

When that lady came before Christ there in that synagogue, she was made whole. And when you come before Him, no religious rules or ecclesiastical limits can bar you from the blessings or the freedom of a redeemed, royal daughter in God's divine household.

Tradition Can Traumatize

If you have been traumatized or censored by religious rulers; if tradition has you bent and bound, it is time for you to respond to Christ's call to dignity and to destiny. Gather your forces; muster your courage and march toward Him.

When you make contact with Him, your shackles will dissolve whether they are religious, psychological, physical or spiritual. Woman, be free, in the name of Jesus. Be lifted from tradition to freedom.

Christ sets you free from negative thoughts, from guilt, from self-condemnation, from feelings of inferiority, from timidity and mediocrity, from fear, from anxiety and from depression.

A young prostitute came to one of our meetings. She had sold her body to support her drug habit. She had been in and out of prison but institutional correction had never changed her.

When that young woman heard the gospel, she discovered new purpose for her life. She accepted Jesus as her personal Savior and her life was completely transformed. Then she set out on a mission of love to lead other self-destructive people to Jesus Christ.

What a transformation takes place when a life is touched by the Lord. He forgives, He heals and He restores a person in just a moment of time. Religion cannot do this, but Jesus can — and He will.

Woman, you are loosed from your infirmity. That is what He announces to you — today.

1.	Lu.13:12	3.	Jn.8:36
2.	Ac.1:8	4.	Jn.8:32

"Jesus is your liberator and your friend. He gives you pardon and He gives you peace; He gives you pride and He gives you purpose. He makes you a Woman Without Limits."

Chapter 23

JESUS, WOMAN'S LIBERATOR

IN THE SYNAGOGUE on that Sabbath day, the people could see the difference between religion and love at work. They could make a choice. They could follow religion which saw only the importance of a rule, or they could accept Jesus who saw the broken human person of the bent woman and who took the initiative to make her whole.

Basically, those are the same options we have today — religion or Jesus. They represent different worlds. They lead to different destinies. One leads to death, the other to life.

Jesus said: *I am the way, the truth, and the life.*[1] *Whoever has God's Son has life; whoever does not have his Son, does not have life.*[2]

The ruler of the synagogue reacted to Christ healing the poor woman's bent back on the Sabbath. Jesus countered his reaction by calling him a *hypocrite.* Then He asked: *Does not each of you on the Sabbath loose your ox or ass from the stall and lead it away to water?*

And ought not this woman, whom Satan has bound for eighteen years be loosed from this bondage on the Sabbath day?[3]

This synagogue ruler was outwardly concerned about religion, but inwardly he was an insensitive person. He had more concern for an animal than he did for a female person created in God's image.

Resisting Restrictions

The point of Christ's action that day in the synagogue was to illustrate that you need never bow or submit to outdated ecclesiastical ordinances or to chauvinistic dogmas or rules which demean your personhood or which discredit your individual value as a human person.

Never question the fact that you, as a woman, are special. You are a unique creation of your heavenly Father.

Jesus is your liberator and your friend. He is your Savior and your healer. He is your provider and your protector. He is your peace and your life.

Jesus gives you pardon and He gives you peace. He gives you pride and He gives you purpose. He makes you a *Woman Without Limits*.

The attitudes of other people can never demean you nor deprecate your value, unless you permit them to. It is your attitude that counts.

After the woman in the synagogue was set free, I believe she became one of those who followed Jesus as He went from town to town, showing the multitudes how much God loved them.

Freedom for You

Now, you too have heard the liberating words of Jesus and you too have been brought from tradi-

tion to freedom.   You can rise; you can stand up
with pride, loosed forever from the bondage of outdated religious customs and bigoted rules.   You are
freed from inferiority, from timidity and from a
sense of worthlessness.

You are valuable.   You are a Jesus-person.
Your life now has new and exciting dimensions of
hope and of happiness, of forgiveness and of fulfillment, of peace and of purpose.

Now that you have accepted His love for you,
*no good thing will He withhold from those that walk
uprightly before Him.*[4]

God loves you.   As His friend and partner,
share Christ's love with others.   Always remember:
As you reach out to bless people, God reaches out
to bless you.

1.   Jn.14:6   3.   Lu.13:15-16
2.   1Jn.5:12   4.   Ps.84:11

Daisy meets with Nigerian Governor
and state officials in a crusade
planning session. She sits with
an African king to witness to him
of Christ through an interpreter
(kneeling in foreground).

PART V

FINANCIAL SECURITY
FOR
WOMEN

IT IS NOT God's will for any woman to live in sin or guilt, in disease or suffering, in failure or poverty.

There was only one time in the Bible when God called on His people to prove Him — and that concerned their money.

We had been taught that God was spiritual; that money was carnal; that we should beware of it and never desire it; that the only way we could be humble and submissive to God's will was to be poor.

The facts of the Bible are that God has provided for those who trust in Him spiritual freedom, physical health and material wealth so that His children can be partners with Him in giving the gospel to others.

There can be no loving without giving, no giving without receiving, no planting without reaping.

The Bible foundation for financial security for women is as solid as it is for men. From the day I discovered this truth, I looked at money from God's point of view. I knew that I must share this vital information with every woman I could reach, throughout the world.

Chapter 24

THE UNCHANGING LAW

THE GREATEST guarantee for financial security for women is to accept and to practice God's law of sowing and reaping.

We can predict our own circumstances tomorrow by the seeds we sow today.

Our seeds are our thoughts, our words and our deeds or actions.

Sooner than we imagine, our own seeds materialize themselves around us. It is the principle of sowing and reaping and it applies to every aspect of life — for women exactly the same as for men.

In the Bible, Paul said: *Whatever you sow, that shall you also reap.*[1] That applies to you as a woman.

The Unchanging Principle

Early in the Bible, God gave us an unchanging law: *While the earth remains, seedtime and harvest shall not end.*[2] This is a fundamental of life — giving to receive. It is what God did to save us. *God so loved that He gave.*[3]

When we love in deed and in action, we are planting seeds that will return to us a harvest in whatever form of love we have sown.

Let us not love in word, neither in tongue; but in deed and in truth.[4]

What we think about, talk about, and do, is our way of planting the seeds that will materialize of their kind around us and within us, and that is the principle that makes you another *Woman Without Limits.*

It is impossible to plant without reaping, to love without being loved, to give without receiving.

Extend kindness and receive kindness. Show mercy and receive mercy. Give, and receive more of what you give. Sow, and reap more of what you plant.

God's law for a prosperous, happy, successful life is that you as a woman, can choose to plant good seeds; then you as a woman, will reap an abundant return of good blessings.

1.   Ga.6:7   3.   Jn.3:16
2.   Ge.8:22   4.   1Jn.3:18

Chapter 25

TWO WORDS THAT CHANGED
OUR LIVES

GOD'S ABUNDANT LIFESTYLE grows out of the fertile seedbed of faith in Jesus Christ and of total trust in Him. He wants us to prove that He is real, and that His promises are trustworthy. He wants us to put them to the test.

I shall never forget the day my husband and I learned this principle. We knew that it is as certain for women as it is for men.

This unusual experience with God occurred during a financial crisis in our world ministry. This story will help you to grasp God's law of financial security for women.

We had over-extended our evangelism commitments abroad. Our major outreaches overseas, such as our national conferences, our mass crusades, our soulwinning seminars and our tools for evangelism airlifts, are planned far in advance.

It sometimes takes months to negotiate large printing contracts; to get tools dispatched and to plow through the red tape of getting equipment through foreign customs offices; to plan a campaign, a great training seminar, or a special conference; or to tie the ends for a big national gospel saturation.

We had committed ourselves to a heavy schedule in several countries and as those responsibilities came due almost at the same time, we did not have the funds to meet our commitments.

Satan accused us and said: "You think you have faith? You say you are doing the thing nearest God's heart — reaching the unreached? Where is your God — and where are your partners? You have given priority to the unreached, but your God has abandoned you."

When we looked at our financial accounts, we decided to fast and pray for a week, to listen for God's direction.

Our Crisis — Our Answer

The Lord spoke to us. Each of us experienced the awareness of His presence as He spoke to us from the scriptures. T.L. says that he actually heard these words spoken audibly to him: "Prove me. Prove me now!"

So we searched for every scripture where God told someone to prove Him.

To our amazement, there was only one verse in the Bible where God called on His people to prove Him — and that concerned their money.

Money was our problem. The only way we could fulfill our commitments was with money. The devil had accused us about money. He had incriminated God for being unconcerned about souls because money was lacking.

We realized: Christ gave the Great Commission.   Then He assigned Christians to carry it out. Some would *go;*[1] others would *send.*[2]   People are His agents to do His work.   But money is always needed to do His work among people.

God places people here on earth and makes them stewards of all that He provides — possessions, houses, lands, money.   It is all entrusted to people, in order that He may prove them as His stewards.

Then He says to them: *Bring all the tithes* (at least one-tenth of your money) ... *and prove Me now in this ... if I will not open for you the windows of heaven, and pour out for you such blessing that there will not be room enough to receive it.*[3]

God tells us to bring to Him our money and to prove Him as our provider.   In return, He proves His covenant by returning to us more money than we bring to Him, so that we may bring back more to Him and receive yet a bigger portion.

Jesus reconfirmed this principle by telling us — women believers as well as men believers: *Give, and it will be given to you: good measure, pressed down, shaken together, and running over...*[4]

When I realized that the only time God ever asked us to put Him to the test was with our money, it really affected me as a woman.   I had never considered money in a spiritual way.

We had been taught that money was carnal; that God was spiritual; that we should beware of money and never desire it; that the only way we could be humble and submissive to God's will was to be poor.

That day as we prayed, neither of us knew that the only verse in the Bible where God said, *Prove me!*, was about money.

1.   Mk.16:15   3.   Mal.3:10
2.   Ro.10:15   4.   Lu.6:38

Chapter 26

MONEY REPRESENTS LIFE

FOR THE FIRST TIME, T.L. and I began to see money like God sees it — as a blessing, as a tool to be used in His work among people.

Years ago, we heard Billy Graham preach about money. He said: "Money represents your life in the form of currency."

From that day, I began to realize that God promises financial security for women as well as for men. I knew He was showing me this truth so that I could help women around the world to learn how to have financial security of their own, and how they could learn to be part of God's plan for blessing people.

With so many single-parent homes, with working women in leadership, in politics, in business, in banking, in industry and in every phase of life, it is time for each woman believer to discover that God's laws for financial security are not sexual or social; that they are for women and men alike, in every nation and in every culture.

When you are paid a salary, or gain money from an investment, from a business or from your industry in any field, that money represents the period of your life that was required to earn it or to produce it. You will never live that part of your life again. That salary or dividend or financial increase or profit or the earnings you receive represents a portion of your life in the form of currency.

That is why money is valued next to life itself. It is the most treasured material possession in life. People guard their money more than anything else, except their life. Jesus said, *Where your treasure is, there will your heart be also.*[1]

You now understand why God says in essence: *Bring your money to Me and put Me to the test with it.*

God is saying: If you trust Me with your dearest material possession, that is proof that you trust Me with your life.

Money From God's Viewpoint

From the beginning of time, people with faith in God have consecrated to Him the offerings of their best.[2] The Bible calls it firstfruits[3] — their first and their best for God's work.[4]

There can be little faith in God that does not touch your money. What you do with it is what you do with your life. What you really believe in is proven by where you put your money.[5]

So God asks you to put Him to the test with your most treasured material possession, to prove that you trust Him with your most precious spiritual possession — your life.[6]

Then He promises to return to you abundantly more than you trusted Him with, as proof that He is real and that His promises are valid.

Honor the Lord with your possessions (material things), *and with the firstfruits* (the first and the best) *of all your increase; So your barns will be filled with plenty.*[7]

That is God's law of financial security for women the same as it is for men.

My whole attitude about money changed when I began to see it from God's point of view. I knew that I must share this vital foundation for financial security with every woman I could reach, throughout the world.

I knew that some might criticize me for talking or writing about financial security for women. But I also knew that my critics would only be those who either wanted to restrain women to a subservient role, or they would be those who *love their money*[8] too much to prove God with it.

I began to teach the promises of God concerning His material blessings, to help Christians — both women and men, to accept God's attitude about money and to liberate them from the traditional biased and negative attitude which religion generally fosters about material prosperity — especially for women.

Women around the world — as well as men, must be taught God's will concerning material blessings. Only then can they exercise their faith for God's best in their lives — materially as well as spiritually.

God wants His daughters as well as His sons to see that *it is He who gives them power to get*

wealth.[9]   *Riches and wealth are the gift of God.*[10]
*The Lord has pleasure in the prosperity of His ser-
vant.*[11]   He wishes *above all things that you may
prosper.*[12]

These promises are for every believer. Since
Faith comes by hearing the word of God,[13] I am
sharing later in this book a list of Bible quotations
to create faith in your heart for God's material
blessings in your life.

He says in essence, *Bring your money and
prove Me with it. Put Me to the test. See how I will
return a harvest greater than you sowed and your
barns will overflow with plenty.*

These promises — and many others, are the
foundation for faith for financial security for
women the same as for men.

God guarantees that when you as a woman,
plant by reaching out to others, you will reap as
God reaches out to you.[14]

1.	Lu.12:34	3.	2Ch.31:5	8.	1Ti.6:10
2.	Ge.4:3-4		Ne.10:35-37	9.	De.8:18
	Ge.8:20	4.	Ex.22:29-30	10.	Ec.5:19
	Ge.22:9-14		Ex.23:19	11.	Ps.35:27
	Ex.12:5	5.	Mt.6:21	12.	3Jn.1:2
	Le.22:21	6.	Mk.8:36-37	13.	Ro.10:17
	Nu.18:12	7.	Pr.3:9-10	14.	Lu.6:38

Chapter 27

PROSPERITY FOR WOMEN

GOD CREATED WOMAN and man for an abundant lifestyle.

It is not His will that we should live a life of sin and guilt, of disease and suffering, of failure and poverty. One is no more God's will than the other.

The entire Bible is God's revealed plan of complete and full salvation for the whole person, spiritually, physically and materially.

Blessed be the Lord, who daily loads us with benefits, even the God of our salvation.[1]

The Bible says: *Beloved* (daughters), *I wish above all things that you may prosper, and be in health even as your soul prospers.*[2] (*Prosper,* in the original Greek, clearly includes financial blessing.)

All the wealth of the world is created by our Father. The gold and the silver, the oil and the minerals, the precious stones and the fields, the flocks and the herds; they are all the creation of our Father. He owns it all.[3] Women as well as men, are created to be temporary stewards of the earth's wealth.

Basics For Women

Here are two basic facts about God's plan for your financial security as a *Woman Without Limits:*

1.   Your Father created all of the wealth on this earth and it is His. He can and will place it in your hands for His work's sake as you claim His promises and act upon His success principles with faith.

2.   Your Father wills that you experience financial prosperity for His glory and for His work. Poverty is no more God's will for His children than sickness or oppression or any other thing that hinders or limits personal happiness, security, self-esteem or fulfillment in life as a human person with dignity.

Birds, Lilies and You

God knows your height.[4] He has numbered the hairs of your head.[5] Every sparrow is counted,[6] and He is concerned about each need you have.[7] He feeds the birds and clothes the lilies[8] and it is His will that you live in abundance.[9]

God's plan for you as a woman, is that you be saved, blessed, happy, healthy, prosperous, successful and wise.

The world of plenty all about you is ample proof that your heavenly Father wants you to live in abundance.   God created enough so that every woman as well as every man can enjoy all that is needed or desired.

Religious tradition infers that it is God's will for His daughters to be impoverished, acquiescent, deprecated and insignificant. But there is nothing in the Bible to indicate that a believing woman should live in poverty and self-abasement in order to manifest humility and godliness.

The facts of the Bible are that God has provided for every believer, both male and female, individual dignity, spiritual freedom, physical health and material prosperity so that His children can be partners with Him in giving the gospel to others.

Part of God's blessing which He covenants to give to all who *obey the voice of the Lord* is that He *will grant you plenty of goods.*[10]

Jesus came *that you might have life and that you might be in abundance.*[11]

1.	Ps.68:19	4.	Lu.12:25	8.	Lu.12:27-28
2.	3Jn.1:2	5.	Mt.10:30	9.	Jn.10:10
3.	Ex.19:5	6.	Lu.12:6	10.	De.28:1,11
	Le.25:23	7.	Ps.31:19	11.	Jn.10:10 FB
	Ps.50:10-11		Is.64:4		
	Hag.2:8		Ph.4:19		

Daisy Osborn is awarded honorary doctorates (above) at Zoe College in Florida, and (below) at Bethel Christian College in California.

Chapter 28

PROMISES FOR PROSPERITY

IT SEEMS ALMOST incredible that religious tradition could overlook so many promises of material prosperity for women or men who believe God's word.

Riches and wealth are the gift of God.[1]

Blessed is the one who fears the Lord, who delights in his commandments. Wealth and riches shall be in their house.[2]

The Lord has pleasure in the prosperity of His servants.[3] That means you — and it means financial security for women.

No good thing will He withhold from them that walk uprightly.[4]

That I may cause those that love me to inherit wealth; and I will fill their treasures.[5]

Observe to do according to (My word) *that you may prosper wherever you go.*[6]

Keep the words of this covenant, that you may prosper in all that you do.[7]

Walk in God's ways, so that you may prosper in all that you do, and wherever you turn yourself.[8]

The Lord shall make you plenteous in goods.[9]

The blessing of the Lord, it makes rich.[10]

The Lord is my shepherd, I shall not want.[11]

They that seek the Lord shall not want any good thing.[12]

Blessed be the Lord, who daily loads us with benefits.[13]

Seek first the kingdom of God (the expansion of God's kingdom worldwide) *and all these things shall be added to you.*[14]

He wills that you may prosper wherever you go, that you make your way prosperous, and that you have good success.[15]

The Lord shall make you prosperous in goods. The Lord shall open to you his good treasure, to bless all the work of your hand.[16]

You shall eat in plenty and be satisfied and praise the name of the Lord your God, that has dealt wondrously with you.[17]

God has given riches and wealth and power to rejoice in your labor; this is the gift of God.[18]

Let the Lord be magnified, which has pleasure in the prosperity of his servants.[19]

Wealth and riches shall be in your house.[20]

With You is the fountain (source) *of life.*[21]

Both riches and honor come of You.[22]

O Lord, the earth is full of Your riches.[23]

Believe in the Lord your God, so shall you prosper.[24]

Those that seek Me early shall find Me. Riches and honor are with them.[25]

The wealth of the earth is our Father's. *The silver is Mine, and the gold is Mine.*[26] *All the earth is Mine.*[27] *The land is Mine.*[28] *Every beast of the forest is Mine, and the cattle on a thousand hills.*[29]

God clearly shows that His will is for His daughters as well as His sons to inherit *good land, to eat good things, to build goodly houses; for your herds and flocks to multiply and your silver and gold to be multiplied.*[30]

For Women Too

This is His will for you as a woman, as well as it is His will for any man.

Remember the Lord your God: For it is He that gives you power to get wealth.[31]

He said, *Honor the Lord with the firstfruits of all your increase: So shall your barns be filled with plenty.*[32]

God says to bring your tithes and offerings to Him and *prove Me now with this, if I will not open you the windows of heaven, and pour you out a blessing that there shall not be room enough to receive it.*[33]

Jesus said: *Give, and it shall be given to you: good measure, pressed down, and shaken together, and running over. For with the same measure that you use, it shall be used to measure to you again.*[34]

Give and it shall be given to you is as true for a woman as *Ask and you shall receive.*[35]

God created an abundance of everything. He placed you here amidst it all.

God is able to give you everything you need and more, so that there will not only be enough for your own needs, but plenty left over to give joyfully to others.

For God, who gives to the farmer to plant, and later on, good crops to harvest and eat, will give you more and more seed to plant and will make it grow so that you can give away more and more fruit from your harvest.

Yes, God will give you much so that you can give away much, and when you take your gifts to those who need them they will break out into thanksgiving and praise to God for your help.[36]

My God shall supply all your needs.[37]

Purpose of Material Plenty

It is time for Christian women as well as men to look upon material prosperity objectively. I cannot imagine a committed believer seeking material wealth for wealth's sake alone.

Material abundance is to be regarded as 1) a

blessing for your own life, 2) as a medium for God's work on earth, and 3) as a resource for sharing the gospel *with every creature.*

Enter a faith partnership with God to prosper financially for two reasons: 1) In order to live the abundant lifestyle which God wills for you,[38] and most importantly, 2) In order to be able to share the gospel with *all the world.*

A woman who is enterprising and who becomes materially successful, such as the Proverbs woman,* can promulgate the gospel to her world as much as a successful man can.

God's will is to bless you as a woman, with His material abundance, to the degree that you plant of that abundance in the fertile soil of His work for blessing people. That is the solid foundation for financial security for women — or for anyone.

Whatever a woman sows, that shall she also reap.[39]

While the earth remains, seedtime and harvest shall not end.[40]

Heaven and earth shall pass away, but God's word shall not pass away.[41]

A Christian woman's financial security tomorrow is the sure harvest of her financial planting today. And God's law is not sexual. It applies to every woman as well as it does to every man.

---

*Be sure to get my book, *The Woman Believer.* The Proverbs woman is dealt with in chapter 21.

See money from God's viewpoint. As you
reach out to bless others with the gospel through
planting your first and your best in His work, He
will reach out to you to crown your life with His
blessings of abundance because He regards you as a
Woman Without Limits.

1.	Ec.5:19	15.	Jos.1:5-9	29.	Ps.50:10
2.	Ps.112:1,3	16.	De.28:11-12	30.	De.8:7-13
3.	Ps.35:27	17.	Jl.2:26	31.	De.8:18
4.	Ps.84:11	18.	Ec.5:19	32.	Pr.3:9-10
5.	Pr.8:21	19.	Ps.35:27	33.	Mal.3:10
6.	Jos.1:7	20.	Ps.112:1,3	34.	Lu.6:38
7.	De.29:9	21.	Ps.36:9	35.	Jn.16:24
8.	1K.2:3	22.	1Chr.29:12	36.	2Co.9:10-11 LB
9.	De.28:11	23.	Ps.104:24	37.	Ph.4:19
10.	Pr.10:22	24.	2Chr.20:20	38.	Jn.10:10
11.	Ps.23:1	25.	Pr.8:17-18	39.	Ga.6:7
12.	Ps.34:10	26.	Hag.2:8	40.	Ge.8:22
13.	Ps.68:19	27.	Ex.19:5	41.	Mt.24:35
14.	Mt.6:33 RV	28.	Le.25:23		

PART VI

FAITH
TO
LIVE
BY

THE GREATEST THING that can happen to you as a woman, is to discover your own self-value, your value to people and your value to God and to His plan for your life.

You discover these vital facts in the Bible — God's word — which is the only source of real faith to live by.

All over the world, I have helped thousands of precious people who were unsaved and afraid of God, to discover why Jesus died on the cross, and how his sacrifice opened the way for them to come to God and to be His friends and partners in life.

God is Spirit. You are His body, His hands to touch with, His eyes to see through, His feet to walk with, His heart to love through, His ears to hear with, His arms to embrace with.

How does Jesus Christ live today?

He lives through you.

Here are the five questions that will unlock the way to God and to His happy, healthy, successful lifestyle that He wants every woman — every human person, to enjoy.

Chapter 29

THE OPEN WAY FOR WOMEN

GOD HIMSELF PROVED how much He esteems woman, by the price He paid to redeem her — the price of the life of His Son, Jesus Christ. His act of love ends all argument about any woman's divine worth as a person.

Once you discover the esteem which God has for you and the value which He places upon you, then you are ready for the most powerful and dynamic experience any person can ever receive.

You are ready to associate or to relate yourself — to hook up and to identify yourself — with God in a personal encounter that will mark you for as long as you live.

This will be powerful news because it is what opens the gates to God's riches, health, success and abundance.

Here are the five questions that will unlock the way to God and to His happy, healthy, successful lifestyle that He wants every woman — every human person — to enjoy:

1) Who is Jesus Christ? 2) Why did He come? 3) Why was He put to death? 4) Why did He come back from the dead? 5) How does He live today?

A Woman's Way to God

True success and true happiness begins by discovering the way to God. You as a woman were created in His image, to be His friend and partner in life. He never planned for you to be alienated from Him or for you to occupy an inferior role in His royal family.

When Adam and Eve sinned in the garden of Eden, the sentence of death came on them both because God had said, *The soul that sins shall die.*[1]

The way into God's presence was barred forever to women as well as to men who did not believe His word. The Bible says, *Your iniquities have separated between you and your God; your sins have hid His face from you.*[2]

But God so loved the world — you included — *that He gave His only begotten Son, that whoever believes in Him shall not perish but have everlasting life.*[3]

That is why Jesus said, *I am the way, the truth and the life.*[4] He came from God to assume all of your sins and to endure the punishment you deserved so that you could stand before God justified and restored to Him as though no sin had ever been committed.[5]

Jesus is every woman's way to God.

In Old Testament times, God's presence was only manifested in the Holy Place of the Tabernacle or of the temple.[6] Only the high priest could enter that restricted place where God manifested

His presence, and he could only do it once a year, and then only with a blood offering both for his own sins and for the sins of the people.[7]

If anyone other than that high priest entered God's presence in the Holy Place, that person would die,[8] which illustrates that people could not come into God's presence. The way was barred because of sin in the human race.

But when Jesus Christ shed His blood and died for our sins, that great veil in the Temple which separated the people from the presence of God, was torn apart from top to bottom,[9] illustrating that since our sins have been punished, the way to God is now wide open to everyone who believes on Jesus Christ — Jews or Gentiles, priests or lay persons, women or men, servants or property owners.

As you read this book, God will make this truth real to you. Deep in your heart you will know that Jesus is the Son of God, the one sent to be your sacrifice[10] and who gave His life as a substitute for your sins.[11]

The Bible tells us, in essence, that *the blood of Jesus Christ, God's Son, was shed for the remission of your sins.*[12]

When you think of the blood of Christ, remember that it is the proof that your substitute has been offered and His life has been laid down, for you.[13]

The blood of Jesus stands as evidence that He became your sacrifice.[14]   He assumed your sins.[15]

He endured your judgment.[16]

Christ's blood has been honored before God as proof that the penalty of death for your sins has been paid — not by you, but by your substitute, Jesus Christ.[17]

God loved you too much to let you die and face eternal judgment for your sins.[18]   Christ bore them all for you, in your name.

Now that your sins have been punished, there is no more punishment to be endured.[19]   You are free![20]   You are saved — the moment you believe on Jesus Christ.[21]

Believe on the Lord Jesus Christ and you shall be saved.[22]

Being justified by faith (in Jesus Christ) *you now have peace with God through our Lord Jesus Christ.*[23]

There is therefore no condemnation to them that are in Jesus Christ.[24]

When you believe on Jesus Christ, you shall not come into condemnation (or judgment for your sins), *but you are passed from death into life.*[25]

That is who Jesus Christ is!

He is your way back to God.[26]   The Bible says, *When you have Jesus, the Son of God, you have life.*[27]   *Christ is your life.*[28]

It is vital that you have personal faith — right

now — that Jesus Christ is the Son of God, that
He lived as your example, that He shed His own
blood, gave His own life, and died as your substitute, and that He did it to absolve you of all guilt
before God.   That is the gospel — the good news
of salvation!   That is what makes you a *Woman
Without Limits*.

I stated five questions at the beginning of this
chapter.   Now you are beginning to understand the
answers to those questions.

1.	Eze.18:4,20	7.	Ex.30:10	15.	1Pe.2:24
2.	Is.59:2		He.9:7-8	16.	Is.53:3
3.	Jn.3:16	8.	Ex.28:34-35	17.	He.9:12-14
4.	Jn.14:6	9.	Mt.27:51 LB		Col.1:14
5.	1Pe.2:24	10.	He.9:26	18.	2Pe.3:9
	2Co.5:21		Ga.1:4	19.	He.10:18-21
	Ro.5:1		Ep.5:2		Eze.18:32
	Ro.5:8-11		Tit.2:14	20.	Jn.8:32,36
	Ro.8:1-4	11.	2Co.5:21		Ga.5:1
	Ro.8:15-17		He.2:9	21.	Ac.2:21
	Ep.2:4-10		1Pe.2:24	22.	Ac.16:31
	Ep.2:13-14		1Pe.3:18	23.	Ro.5:1
	Col.1:13	12.	Mt.26:28	24.	Ro.8:1
	Col.1:21-23		1Jn.1:7	25.	Jn.5:24
	Col.2:13-15	13.	Ro.5:9	26.	He.10:20
	Col.3:10 LB	14.	He.9:14	27.	1Jn.5:12
6.	Ex.25:8,22		1Pe.1:19	28.	Col.3:4

THE JESUS LIFE

Christ is alive! He now reigns in our hearts.
　He called us! He filled us! He set us apart.
His truth and His grace were the seeds of our start.
　His love energizes the life we impart.

He sent us to give the good news to the poor;
　To tell all the captives, they're prisoners no more;
To announce to the blind that their sight is restored;
　To lift the down-trodden; they're free evermore.

As the Father sent Jesus to show forth His will.
　Now Jesus sends us to reveal Him, until
Everyone hears that, of His own free will,
　Christ died to redeem them, to heal every ill.

So now that God's Kingdom in us is the key;
　Our reason on earth is to let Jesus be
The same in our flesh; He lives to set free
　Whoever believes the good news. Let it be!

By Daisy and her husband T.L.

Chapter 30

WHO IS JESUS CHRIST?

WHAT I HAVE SHARED with you in the previous chapter, gives you the answer to the vital question: Who is Jesus Christ. May God help you, right now, to say from your heart what Martha said: *Lord, I believe that You are the Christ, the Son of God, who should come to this world.*[1]

Paul said, *For if you tell others* (confess) *with your own mouth that Jesus Christ is your Lord, and if you believe in your own heart that God raised Him from the dead, you will be saved. For it is by believing in your heart that you become right with God; and with your mouth you tell others of your faith, confirming* (or giving proof of) *your salvation.*[2]

Those verses in the Bible show you how very vital it is for you to really know who Jesus Christ is, and that you believe on Him enough to speak of Him to others, as Paul said: *Wherever we go we talk about Christ to all who will listen.*[3]

When Jesus came into Caesarea Philippi, he asked his disciples, who do people say that I, the Son of Man, am?[4]

Their answers indicated confusion. Some thought He was this or that prophet, but Peter said, *You are the Christ, the Son of the living God.*[5]

Jesus blessed Peter for this answer and said that only God could have revealed it to him. Then

He added: *Upon this rock* (the revelation that Jesus is the Son of the living God) *will I build My church, and the gates of Hades cannot prevail against it.*[6]

For you, as a woman, to discover true faith to live by, your faith-life can only begin by believing that Jesus Christ is God's Son, your substitute who died in your place so that you can come back and live in God's presence.

That is the way to peace, happiness, serenity, health and success.

| 1. | Jn.11:27 | 3. | Col.1:28 LB | 5. | Mt.16:16 |
| 2. | Ro.10:9-10 LB | 4. | Mt.16:13 | 6. | Mt.16:18 |

Chapter 31

WHY DID JESUS COME?

OUR SECOND QUESTION concerns the purpose of Christ coming to this world. *He came* to seek and to save you and me. When I consider the price that He paid to find me and to restore me to God, I begin to realize my infinite value to Him.

The Son of Man is come to seek and to save that which is lost.[1]

Jesus said, *I am come that you might have life, and that you might have it in abundance.*[2]

In Mark, Chapter 2, a leper came to Jesus. He touched him and His divine life made the leper as clean as a child.

What Christ did for that poor leper exemplifies the purpose of His mission to save and to bless humanity.

Lepers Healed Today

My husband and I have seen lepers healed around the world — notable lepers, and their healing has affected thousands of lives and has helped many people to *believe on the Lord Jesus Christ.*[3]

We received a wonderful letter from the president of a Bible School. He wrote us to share a testimony given to their student body by a gospel minister who had just attended one of our crusades:

"I witnessed marvelous healings in the Osborn Crusade. I know personally of six lepers who were completely healed after prayer. First, they said the awful burning sensation in their bodies had stopped.

"Then later, I saw them and their leprous skin had changed. It was like a child's — so clean and beautiful. The leprosy was completely gone and also the disfigurements had disappeared from all six of those I followed up on.

"There were other lepers healed in the Osborn Crusade, but I only have personal knowledge of these six, as they were the only ones I checked up on firsthand."

Leprosy is no different than any other sickness in God's sight. Jesus said, *The things which are impossible with people are possible with God.*[4]

Jesus came to *seek and to save* people, and that is the purpose of His ministry today.

Power of Christ's Word

In Matthew, Chapter 8, a centurion talked to Christ about his servant who was near death. Jesus spoke to the man and assured him that His servant was healed. The life of Christ's words healed the man. He came to help and to heal people.

He said, *The words that I speak to you are spirit and they are life.*[5]

To show the power of Christ's words, the

Bible says that *as Jesus was teaching ... the power of the Lord was present to heal the people.*[6]

All over the world my husband and I have witnessed the power of the Lord healing the people as we have preached. Cripples have walked, the deaf have heard, the blind have received sight and all kinds of miracles have taken place as we have spoken and taught the promises of Christ to the people. We have proven around the world that His words, spoken or preached by a woman or a man are the same.

The Maria Teresa Miracle

I was preaching one afternoon to over 200,000 people in our great National Women's Miracle Day rally. As I preached, Maria Teresa who had been crippled, was miraculously healed. The life of God's word healed her. Christ came to save people.

She had been sent home from the hospital to die, with no hope of ever walking again. Several operations on her spine had left her worse than before. She prayed to die.

Then news came of our crusade. She was carried and laid on the ground among the mass of people. I preached about the woman bent double by a "spirit of infirmity".[7] (See Part II of this book.)

Maria had rolled and agonized on the ground, in physical anguish and excruciating suffering.

When I announced Christ's words, *Woman, be free!*, Maria thought that it thundered and that a bolt of lightning had struck her. (In John 12:29, the people thought it thundered when the Lord spoke.) She was shocked to her feet, and healed, but was blinded by God's power that came upon her. She was stunned and she screamed in fear. People thought that she was insane and was having a convulsion.

My husband went into the crowd and brought her to me on the platform as I was preaching, and as soon as I embraced her, her sight was restored, and she realized that she had been healed. She shouted, jumped and danced all over the platform, and the multitude of people was astounded.

Now you understand why Jesus came. He came to give life to every person who will believe on Him. He will give you His miracle life too.

1.	Lu.19:10	4.	Lu.1:37	6.	Lu.5:12
2.	Jn.10:10		Je.32:17,27	7.	Lu.13:11;17
3.	Ac.16:31	5.	Jn.6:63		

Chapter 32

WHY WAS CHRIST PUT TO DEATH?

QUESTION NUMBER THREE is vital to the woman or man who wants to be restored to God. When you comprehend why Christ was crucified, then you can understand why you can be at peace with God. Jesus Christ died for one reason: So that you can live!

The Bible says, *God showed His great love for us by sending Christ to die for us while we were still sinners. ...now He has declared us not guilty.*[1]

Now you belong to Christ Jesus, and though you once were far away from God, now you have been brought very near to Him because of what Jesus Christ has done for you. For Christ Himself is your way of peace.[2]

The Opened Way

All over the world, I have helped thousands of precious people who were unsaved and afraid of God, to discover why Jesus died on the cross, and how His sacrifice opened the way for them to come to God and to be His friends and partners in life.

The wages of sin is death[3] and *the soul who sins shall die.*[4] God's law could not be changed, though He did not want you to die. *I have no pleasure in the death of the one who dies.*[5]   *The Lord is ... not willing that any should perish but that all should come to repentance.*[6]   And that is why *God so loved the world that He gave His only begotten Son, that whoever believes in Him should not perish but have everlasting life.*[7]

Now that Christ died in our place, enduring the judgment and paying the penalty for all of our sins, whoever believes those facts *has everlasting life, and shall not come into judgment, but is passed from death into life.*[8]

Now you understand the answer to the vital third question: Jesus was put to death in our name so that we can have life in His name. *As many as received Him, to them He gave the right to become the children of God, even to those who believe in His name.*[9]

These are written that you may believe that Jesus is the Christ, the Son of God and that believing you may have life in His name.[10]

The moment you believe on Jesus Christ and accept Him as your substitute and Savior, He comes to live in you. You become a new creature. And that is why He was put to death in your place.

If anyone is in Christ, that person is a new creature. Old things are passed away. Everything becomes new.[11]

As we have taught these truths to multitudes of people around the world, we have seen prostitutes and their clients receive Jesus and become clean and new again. Lepers have believed on Him and their flesh has been restored. Blind people have accepted Him and their blind eyes have been healed. Crippled, paralyzed and lame people have received Jesus by faith, and their crippled bodies have been made whole.

Jesus is alive right now, and He wants to come to you — right where you are, now. Only believe, and receive Him as your Savior and Lord.

1.	Ro.5:8-9LB	5.	Eze.18:32	9.	Jn.1:12
2.	Ep.2:13-14LB	6.	2Pe.3:9	10.	Jn.20:31
3.	Ro.6:23	7.	Jn.3:16	11.	2Co.5:17
4.	Eze.18:4,20	8.	Jn.5:24		

Daisy Osborn shares with her husband, T.L., in ministering the love of Christ to nations around the world. She has never been limited by her gender anymore than by her race. They both believe that Christ in a woman is no different than He is in a man. Here, they rejoice together on the final day of another triumphant crusade of evangelism.

Chapter 33

WHY DID JESUS COME BACK FROM THE DEAD?

OUR FOURTH QUESTION holds the secret to the proof of why we can be saved through receiving Jesus Christ. Grasp the significance of why He came back from the dead. Jesus said, *Because I live, you shall live also.*[1]

The Bible says, *God gave us back our lives again when He raised Christ from the dead — only by His undeserved favor have we been saved — and He lifted us up from the grave into glory above with Christ ... all because of what Christ did.*[2]

Before, *we were spiritually dead and doomed by our sins.*[3] *But God is so rich in mercy,* that *He Himself has made us what we are and has given us new lives from Christ Jesus.*[4]

That explains why Jesus Christ came back from the dead, and that is the only true faith to live by.

Because of what Christ did, anyone who hears the Good News about how to be saved, and who trusts Christ, is marked as belonging to Christ ... His presence within us is God's guarantee that He will give us all that He promised.[5] *God has purchased us and He guarantees to bring us to Himself.*[6]

So overflowing is His kindness towards us that

*He took away all our sin through the blood of his Son,
by whom we are saved, and He has showered down
upon us the richness of His grace.*[7]

Why was Christ raised from the dead?

*He died for our sins and rose again to make us
right with God.*[8]   That is why He came back from
the dead.

*When God ... brought Christ back to life again,
you were given His wonderful new life to enjoy.*[9]

*It is the same mighty power that raised Christ
from the dead ... that now helps those who believe
in Him.*[10]

*God has brought you back as His friends ... and
now as a result Christ has brought you into the very
presence of God, and you are standing there before
Him with nothing left against you ... This is the
wonderful news ... and I have the joy of telling it to
you.*[11]

That is the real faith to live by!

The Moslem Cripple

A man who had been crippled by polio for
thirty years, was healed as we ministered this good
news of Jesus Christ to a multitude of people.

Being a Moslem, he never believed on Jesus
Christ as God's Son or that God had raised Him
from the dead.

When he listened to our teaching, he believed on

Christ, and accepted Him by faith into his heart.

His crippled legs were healed and he found himself standing on his own feet for the first time in his adult life. (He had dragged his body with his hands all of his life.) He rushed to the platform to show the people the miracle he had received when he believed on Jesus Christ.

Living Proof

He cried aloud saying, "Just look at me! How could a dead Christ do this to me? Look I am healed! You know me. I was a beggar. I never walked! Now I am healed! Jesus Christ must be alive! Otherwise, how could He do this to me? I always thought He was dead. He must be alive! Look! I am well!"

Jesus came back from the dead because He had completed the work of redemption for you. Now your sins are punished. Your judgment is already borne. There is nothing left against you.

Jesus is alive. You can live by that same miracle life that brought Him back from the dead.[12]

1.	Jn.14:19	5.	Ep.1:13-14 LB	9.	Ro.6:4 LB
2.	Ep.2:5-6 LB	6.	Ep.1:14 LB	10.	Ep.1:19-20 LB
3.	Ep.2:5	7.	Ep.2:7-8 LB	11.	Col.1:21-23 LB
4.	Ep.2:4,10 LB	8.	Ro.4:25 LB	12.	Ro.8:11

Daisy teaches the blessings of the Christ—life to the enormous crowd attending one of the E. African Osborn Crusades. (Below) She poses with Evangelist Patrick Chege and Pastor Samuel Wachira, her faithful Swahili interpreters.

Chapter 34

HOW DOES JESUS LIVE TODAY?

OUR FIFTH QUESTION concerns the most meaningful reality in Christianity. Until we grasp the answers to the question, How does Jesus Christ live today, we miss the whole concept and significance of the Christian faith and lifestyle.

Jesus Christ lives today by expressing Himself and His life in and through people. He lives in you when you believe on Him. That was God's plan from the beginning when He created Adam and Eve. He imparted His life — Himself — to them. He became alive in them. That was His dream and He has never changed.

He created both man and woman in His own image. They were extensions of Himself — of His own life. He reproduced Himself.

But when Adam and Eve sinned in the garden of Eden, violating God's word to them, and ate of the forbidden tree, God could not live with sin, because He is righteous. Adam and Eve came under the jurisdiction of Satan who deceived them. The final penalty was deterioration and death.

They were driven out of God's presence and separated forever from Him, as was all of their offspring, the human race — until Jesus Christ came and assumed our guilt and endured the punishment and the judgment of all of our sins, as our substitute.

When Christ's blood was shed for the remission of our sins, and when He gave His life as
a ransom for us, our sins and our guilt were paid
for. Jesus became our way back to God.

The way was opened for every woman and for
every man to be forgiven and accepted back into
God's family as though no sin had ever been committed. The innocent had paid for the guilty. God
loved us that much.

Life Without Limits

*By the blood of Jesus, He opened a new and liv-
ing way which He consecrated for us, through His
flesh,* and He became our *high priest* so that we
can now *draw near to God with a true heart and full
assurance of faith.*[1]

From the moment Christ shed His divine blood
and died in our place, as our substitute, whoever
believes on Him and receives Him by faith and
confesses Him as their Savior and Lord, is born
again and becomes a new creature with the life of
God restored to them.

Jesus Christ actually comes into that woman or
man and imparts His own life and nature to them.
They become, once again, a child of God — without
limits and He lives in them again. That is how
Jesus Christ lives today — in people who believe on
Him.

*As many as receive Jesus Christ, to them He
gives the power to become children of God.*[2]

That experience is a miracle.

That miracle is for you right now.

Jesus Christ becomes one with you.

The Bible says, *I myself no longer live, but Christ lives in me. And the real life I now have within this body is a result of my trusting in the Son of God who loved me and gave Himself for me.*[3]

The Bible says, *God is a Spirit.*[4]   You and I are now His flesh.[5]

He said, *I will live in you, and walk in you.*[6] That is how Jesus Christ lives today. To emphasize the simplicity and the wonder of this vital fact in Christianity, the next chapter will illuminate your understanding even more.

1.	He.10:19-23	4.	Jn.4:24
2.	Jn.1:12	5.	1Co.6:15,19-20
3.	Ga.2:20 LB	6.	2Co.6:16

As Daisy preaches, this woman who had been crippled by polio since she was seven years old, is instantly healed, removes her brace and shoe, and comes to tell of the miracle she has received.

Chapter 35

GOD IS SPIRIT!
WE ARE HIS FLESH!

THE GREATEST THING that can happen to you as a woman, is to discover your own self-value, your value to people and your value to God and to His plan for your life.

You discover these vital facts in the Bible — God's word — which is the only source of real faith to live by.

Today, Jesus Christ lives in you when you believe in Him. He imparts the life of God in you.

Christ Unchanged in You

The Bible says, *Jesus Christ is the same yesterday, today and forever.*[1] The amazing fact is that this Jesus is the same in you, as He was in Galilee.

The Bible says, *For God is at work within you.*[2]

He is Spirit. You are His body, His hands to touch with, His eyes to see through, His feet to walk with, His heart to love through, His ears to hear with, His arms to embrace with.[3]

How does Jesus Christ live today?

He lives through you.[4]

Christian means "Christ-like".

He so thoroughly removed every trace and con-
sequence of your sins, that when you believe on
Him and receive Him by faith, it is as though you
had never committed sins. Now He can come home
and live in you. Therefore, His dream is un-
changed: He wants to have you near Him as His
friend and partner. Jesus is the way. He paid the
price. Now, when you believe in Him, you are
clean, and God can live in and through you.

1.   He.13:8   3.   1Co.6:19-20   4.   Ga.2:20
2.   Ph.2:13LB   1Co.12:27

Chapter 36

FIVE CONFESSIONS
FOR WOMEN

NOW MAKE THESE five confessions from your heart to the Lord, and believe that He hears you.

First: *Lord Jesus,* I believe that You are the Christ, the Son of the Living God, sent from the Father to redeem me from my sins and to give me Your eternal life.

Second: *Lord Jesus,* I believe that You came to seek and to save me from my confusion, from my sins, from my sicknesses and from my despair, so that You could impart God's divine life to me and make me, once again, His friend and partner, as He originally planned.

Third: *Lord Jesus,* I believe that You died on the cross as my substitute; that You assumed all of my sins and that You endured the condemnation and the judgment of my own transgressions so that there would be nothing left against me, and so that I could be restored to God as His redeemed child.

Fourth: *Lord Jesus,* I believe that You rose from the dead, after having shed Your blood to redeem me from my sins; I believe that Your resurrection proved my justification — that because You live, I can live also by the same life that raised You up; and I accept Your life in me now.

Fifth: *Lord Jesus,* I believe that You have removed every sin that was against me, so that I could be a clean vessel for God to live in and through; I do now, by faith, receive you as my personal Savior and Lord, and I recognize that Your life is in me now. I thank You, Lord. I am saved. I am healed. I am made whole. I have peace in my heart and joy in my soul.

I am now a new *Woman Without Limits*. I am not inferior or second class. I am now qualified by your grace to be Your witness, Your team-worker, Your representative, Your expression in any phase of ministry to which you call or inspire or lead me to serve.

I am now unrestricted, unrestrained and unlimited by my economic and social status, by my race, by my color, and by my gender, because I am created in Your likeness and I am redeemed and restored to You forever. Amen!

Part VII

SELF–ESTEEM
FOR WOMEN

GOD'S LIFE IN A WOMAN means that His power is in her — as immeasurable, as miraculous, as productive, and as unrestrained or unlimited as it is in a man.

As a woman created in God's image and now redeemed, you will no longer permit sermonizers, ecclesiastics, doctrinaires, traditions or culture to negate your worth or to deprecate your standing as a daughter in His royal family.

No longer illiterate, you as a woman can read the Bible for yourself and reappraise your spiritual potential in the light of Christ's redemption.

You need never again feel disqualified or dispensable, inferior or insignificant, inept or inappropriate for any position, ministry or service which you are inspired to fill or to perform in Christ's name.

You are Christ's authorized representative.

You yourself are the only one who can limit Christ at work in and through your life!

Chapter 37

FOUNDATION FOR FULFILLMENT

WHEN AS A WOMAN, you recognize your roots in God and when you see yourself as His intended habitation, you actually experience a new awareness of self-esteem.

People esteem women who have self-respect. They draw strength and inspiration from that kind of woman. That is because a woman like that has discovered self-value and self-dignity which is the basis for a positive, productive lifestyle.

A woman like that begins to think and to talk like those who trusted God in Bible days.

I have synopsized and paraphrased for women the powerful statements in Psalm 91. As a woman, embrace these verses for yourself, knowing that God is making them good in your life — right now. These facts form a solid foundation for real fulfillment in your life.

When you dwell in God's presence, He constantly overshadows you with His mighty power. v.1

God is your refuge and strength. He delivers you from every snare and pestilence. vs. 2-3

He covers you. His truth is your armor. You are not afraid, day or night. Though tragedy strikes all around you, your security is in God.   Nothing destroys Him and He lives in you. vs. 4-9

No evil befalls you.   No plague comes to your dwelling because God is there.   His angels keep charge over you wherever you go.   They even bear you up above any danger that is in your way. vs. 10-12

You are able to walk right over any enemy that intends to injure or destroy you. v. 13

These blessings are because God has set His love upon you and you have set your love upon Him. You know the power of His name and He sets you in a high place. v. 14

When you call upon Him, He answers you.   He is with you in trouble.   He delivers you and honors you.   He satisfies you with long life and shows you His salvation. vs. 15-16

Chapter 38

BORN FOR EXCELLENCE
NOT SUBSERVIENCE

IT IS DIFFICULT for any woman to tolerate life without dignity. She may withdraw into seclusion and close the blinds. She may shut herself out from society, or may lie down in a self-made prison of despair and gradually die, the victim of purposeless abandonment.

The curse of surrender, the cancer of idleness, and the shame of rejection can never develop in women who discover their self-value, their dignity and their potential for success and achievement.

Born for Greatness

You as a woman, are born for significance, not mediocrity. You are created for health, not sickness. You are here for success, not failure. You are saved for evangelization, not isolation. You are empowered for witnessing, not silence. You are designed for esteem, dignity and accomplishment, not dishonor, abuse and bigotry.

When women discover these facts, they actually experience a new awakening — a new consciousness of self-esteem and of self-value.

You become tranquil rather than tense. Confident rather than confused. Directed rather than detoured. Bold rather than bashful. Enthusiastic

rather than exhausted.   Ambitious rather than apa-
thetic.   Self-forgiving rather than self-condemning.

God at Work Through Women

When a woman discovers that God is in her;
when she accepts the fact that she came from Him
and is made like Him, then she becomes the God-
person that she was designed to be.   And that can
begin happening inside of you right now.

When you receive Christ in your life, you actually become another manifestation of God in the
flesh.   Your desires become the expressions of His
desires through you.   Your ambitions become the
result of His ambitions within you.   That is why
*old things have passed away; behold, all things have
become new.*[1]

You become a living miracle with Christ's
power at work in and through you.   You discover
your God-like value.   You begin to think, to talk
and to act like the valued person that He intends
you to be.

As you discover your self-value and learn to
esteem and to appreciate yourself because of Jesus
Christ living in you, you become a positive, uplifting
influence in your own home, in your community and
in your world.

God's Design Unfolds

It is said that Michelangelo began sculpting at
least 44 great statues in solid marble.   But to our
knowledge, he only finished 14 of them, such as the
enormous statue of *David* in Florence, Italy, the

Pieta in Rome's basilica, and his monumental *Moses*.

Just think. At least 30 great works of art, conceived and partially sculpted by that great master artist, were left unfinished. (Fortunately, the huge chunks of partially worked marble are preserved in an Italian museum.)

Some of the massive marble blocs reveal only a hand or a leg or an elbow and shoulder or a foot with toes carved by the famous artist. The total design in the great master artist's mind was never completed.

The rest of the body remains frozen in solid marble, locked up forever, never to be formed into the great Michelangelo's total design.

For some reason God has marked you and caused this book to come into your hands because He has purposed that you are one of His special concepts, and He wills that you become the full expression of His original design for you. To do that, you must experience a new birth of self-worth.

You Are God's Best

The material which God has put into you is the very best. You are pure marble, so to speak, a special woman designed and created by God, in His own image.

The only way His full potential in you as a woman, will fail to be developed is if you fail to see your value and position with Him.

When you demean yourself, or when you allow others to condemn and to negate yourself, you are the one who limits what the Master can produce in you.

Tragedy or Triumph

The greatest tragedy in your life would be for you to live and to die and never to come out of yourself — to never realize the possibilities hidden within you.

The greatest triumph in your life is to discover Christ alive in you and to allow Him to help you to *actually become all that God has had in mind for you to be.*[2]

Embracing Christ as your Lord is embracing the source of your self-esteem, as He becomes the center of your life. This happens when you believe on Him and receive Him by faith.

Believing and Acting

Paul expressed the broad spectrum of Christianity in two simple statements: 1) *If you believe in your heart that God raised Jesus from the dead,* and 2) *if you confess with your mouth that Jesus is your Lord, you shall be saved.*[3]

First: Believe it in your heart. That is your *Faith.*

Second: Confess it with your mouth. Share it with others. That is your *Ministry.*

Discovery Without Limits

No one is too young and no one is too old to receive this self-discovery of self-worth.

David Ben Gurion, founder of the State of Israel, learned French after he was seventy years of age.

The great painter, Titian, was painting master-pieces when he was ninety-eight years old.

You are as young as your dreams, as your new projects, as your new ideas and your new values.

No Age Limit for God's Ability

A ninety-six year old man came in a wheelchair to visit my husband and me at our Tulsa head-quarters church, the *International Gospel Center*, where our daughter, LaDonna Osborn is the pastor. He was holding meetings in the city jail every week and had already led over a hundred people to Jesus Christ.

He wanted a projector and a set of our mass crusade documentary films which contain our mes-sages as they are preached in our crusades, our prayers for the unconverted and for the sick, and the reports of the miracles which take place among the people who receive Christ.

He was going to travel across America to show the films and to tell the people about Jesus. He was not a traditional preacher, but he had God's idea about life and he realized how much God val-ues each individual. At an advanced age, he had personally experienced a new awareness of his own value in God's sight.

He said to us, "I cannot die! I have too much to do. Too many people are lost and need Jesus, and I have to tell them."

Nearing one hundred years of age, he had no time to die. You see, no one is too old — nor is anyone too young.

I was saved at the age of twelve, was married at the age of seventeen, was a Bible teacher and associate pastor at the age of nineteen and was a missionary in India at the age of twenty.

No one is too young. No one is too old. No one is excluded from God's work in any field because of their social or economic status, or because of their race or gender.

Today is your day and God has caused this book to come into your hands to encourage you to discover this vital principle of your infinite value to God and to people.

1.   2Co.5:17
2.   Ro.5:2LB
3.   Ro.10:9

Chapter 39

NO RESTRAINTS FOR WOMEN

FOR THOUSANDS OF years, the way to God's blessings in life has been clearly defined in the Bible. But women do not always accept God's beautiful provisions and promises because of restraints and limits imposed upon them by a patriarchal church culture.

A barrage of discriminating religious doctrines and dogmas constantly deprecate womanhood to a level of second-rate membership in Christ's body, restricting them to carefully prescribed subservient roles in the church.

Modern women, whose equality is an accepted fact in the worlds of science, of medicine, of politics, of economics, of business and of industry, can no longer permit the dignity of their personhood to be demeaned by medieval pronouncements of inferiority and of subjugation by a male dominated hierarchy.

Little more than a century ago, pontificating clergymen were meeting in conferences to elucidate the question of whether or not a female person has a soul.

No Longer Illiterate

Since women are no longer illiterate, it is time for them to read the Bible for themselves, and to reappraise their own spiritual potential in the light of Christ's redemption.

It has not been long since ecclesiastical authorities were quoting the Bible to enhance their pious rhetoric about slavery for the blacks. But when literate blacks read the Bible for themselves, the seeds of freedom germinate and produce their rich harvest. The yoke of subjugation is crushed.

The famous slave, Harriet Tubman, caught the vision of freedom long before *The Emancipation.* She escaped from slavery, found her way to freedom, then headed the famed "Underground Railroad" that helped hundreds of slaves to find freedom. They called her "Moses" and "Old Chariot."

Harriet said: "You can call me 'Moses' or anything you like, but don't call me 'slave' cause I MADE MYSELF A FREE WOMAN!"

She refused to allow the system to demean her personhood, and she went down in history as one of the vital influences that finally brought about an end to the system of indignity for millions of people.

Seeds for Self-Esteem

Today the seeds which produce a new awareness of self-esteem are being planted in the hearts of God's royal daughters on a global scale, and remarkable changes are taking place around the world.

My husband and I are greatly encouraged by the impact which our books and public teachings are making upon woman believers worldwide. As delegates, guests and the general public gather for our conferences or crusades or seminars in various nations of the world, these meetings become life-changing experiences for every woman and man who attends them.

As a woman, decide today that since God created you in His own image and likeness, and since Christ shed His blood to redeem you and to restore you to God, that you have dignity and self-value which no ecclesiastical system, church dogma, doctrine or culture can diminish or deny.

God loves you so much that He paid the supreme price of giving His own Son, Jesus, to redeem you by suffering the penalty for your sins, in your place, and He did it before you even knew you needed it.

Since He loved you that much — even when you were not aware of His goodness, that gives you reason to believe that you have divine value and dignity. That opens the way for your new awareness of your self-esteem and of your self-value in God's plan.

The Unrepressive Voice

Life for women as God designed it for you, is too valuable to miss out on. There is too much for you to be, to have, to enjoy, to do. To resign or to surrender hope is to sin, to degenerate, to die.

Look beyond religious or cultural restraints for women; look deep within your own heart where you yearn for God's lifestyle. It is there, within you, because you are born to be God's royal daughter.

Welcome the voice of love that does not negate and condemn you, or demean and restrain you, but that honestly gives you dignity and equality as God's redeemed, justified, restored daughter, with power and with anointing, with authority and with ability as Christ's fully commissioned ambassador, His representative, His witness and His messenger to all of humankind.

Chapter 40

GOD'S WOMAN

UNDER THE INSPIRATION of God's Spirit, my husband wrote this poem to express the dignity, the ability and the destiny of God's *Woman Without Limits*.

God's Woman

GOD'S WOMAN
  She has been redeemed;

GOD'S WOMAN
  She has new esteem.

She's come alive.
  She's on the rise.
  She has a choice
  She has a voice.

GOD'S WOMAN
  With a mission and a call;

GOD'S WOMAN
  With a vision for us all.

She's anointed. She's a witness
  She's appointed. She is gifted.
  Christ is her identity
  Of dignity and destiny.

The blood of Christ removed her shame
Now she acts in Jesus' name.
The power of the Holy Ghost
Has sent her to the uttermost.

GOD'S WOMAN
Of faith and hope and power.

GOD'S WOMAN,
With life and love THIS HOUR.

By T.L. Osborn

Chapter 41

A WOMAN'S WORTH

AS ONE OF God's women, created in His image with dignity for His service, He wants to share His life in and through you, exactly the same as He does in and through any other person, male or female.

God is the same when He lives in and through you as a woman, as when He expressed Himself through Jesus Christ. God does not change when He comes to live in a woman. His ministry through you is not limited by your race, your social status or your gender.

How God Speaks

Look beyond yourself as a woman, and see God at work in you. Experience a new consciousness of your own value in His plan.

Let your heart leap with new hope. Say:

O Lord, I am created for partnership with You. I respond to this gentle love-voice that brings me good news and that reminds me that I am Your royal daughter — a redeemed member of Your divine household. I am not worthless. I have divine value.

My Father, You believe in me. You think that I am worth everything You paid to redeem me. The dignity of Your nature is in me because You created me. You are giving me a new awareness of self-esteem and of self-worth, so that You can be Yourself and share Yourself in and through me. Thank You, Lord!

Tell God that you have decided to be a full part of His plan, to accept His evaluation of yourself, and to welcome Him to live in and through you.

Prayer

Say this to God: Oh, Lord I have heard Your uplifting voice through this wonderful book. I have decided to be what You want me to be.

I have discovered Your value system for my life. I have learned what a price You paid to prove how much I am worth in Your sight. Your blood was shed to make me clean.[1]

Thank You for valuing me too much to let me die in my sins. Thank You for the power of Your love and of Your life that makes me Your royal daughter, now that I have welcomed You home to live in me.

The blood of Jesus Christ cleanses me.[2] Your life regenerates me.[3] Your joy fills me.[4]

You have made my body Your temple. I am commissioned to represent You in this life to people.[5]

No longer will I demean myself as a woman, nor will I acquiesce to others who demean me.

No longer will I deprecate what You value so highly, nor will I submit to others who deprecate me.[6]

I now realize that I am accepted. I see myself in Your image with Your righteousness and with Your life.

Everything is possible for You at work in me[7] through Jesus Christ my Lord. Amen!

* * *

Now you realize that *Christ in you*[8] is never limited by your social status, by your color, by your race, or by your gender. Christ died for you and He chooses to live in you because you have received Him by faith.

Now you can say with Paul: *I have been crucified with Christ: it is no longer I who live, but Christ lives in me; and the life which I now live in the flesh I live by faith in the Son of God, who loved me and gave himself for me.*[9]

It is the same Jesus who lived in Mary or in Peter or in Phoebe or in Priscilla.

Now God counts on you as His partner to share this truth. You are now one of His co-workers in reaching out to needy people through your own personal rapport with them.

1.	Ro.5:8,9	4.	Jn.15:11	7.	Mk.14:36
2.	1Jn.1:7		Jn.16:24	8.	Ac.10:15
3.	1Pe.1:23	5.	1Co.6:19,20	9.	Ga.2:20
		6.	Ac.10:15		

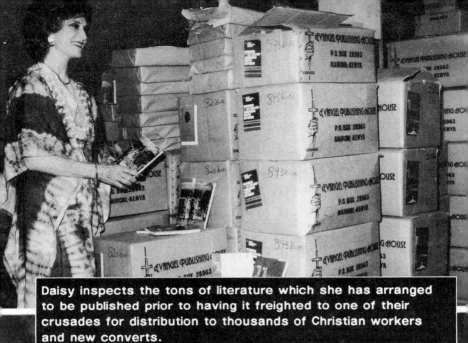

Daisy inspects the tons of literature which she has arranged
to be published prior to having it freighted to one of their
crusades for distribution to thousands of Christian workers
and new converts.

PART VIII

TEAMWORK
WITH
CHRIST

SINCE JESUS CHRIST redeemed all of humanity and sent back the Holy Spirit upon men and women alike, gender is no longer a qualifying factor in God's work.

All believers are to be His representatives, His ambassadors, His voice, His hands, His messengers, His body, His witnesses, His expressions.

But Jewish heritage has been the predominant cultural influence among Christians, and traditions from Biblical times have persistently kept women in the background, repressing and restricting them in God's work.

In today's world, women chauffeur trucks and buses, operate machinery, weld steel, pilot airplanes, captain ships, direct conglomerates; women are entrepreneurs, doctors, teachers, lawyers, judges, politicians; women are governors, senators, judges, provincial commissioners, presidents and prime ministers of nations.

What a waste for religious tradition to repress this enormous world-wide human resource and to restrict women believers to such limited roles of ministry in the church!

It is time for women of God to come down from their feminine pedestals and to take up their crosses as Christ's followers and witnesses — cost whatever it may cost in money or physical effort or religious opposition or persecution. It is time for women to engage themselves in the ministry for which the Holy Spirit rests upon them — witnessing of Jesus and sharing Him with their world.

Chapter 42

GOD'S BEAUTIFUL PLAN

THE PURPOSE OF this book is to encourage every girl, every young lady, every housewife and every woman to take a new look at yourself — to reassess your own value, to reexamine your own faculties and to realize your own unlimited potential in life — as a child of God, redeemed by Jesus Christ and restored to God as His partner and friend.

God has a beautiful plan for you which no one else on earth can fulfill, because you are unique. You are the only one of you that God has.

Women are created to be first-class persons.

First-Class Women

In the church and in God's program, He never designed women to be second-class members with limited expression.

Religious tradition and customs have been relentless in their suppression of the female part of the body of Christ. Those extraordinary women who have overcome feminine subjugation and have dared to do exploits in Christ's name have had little recorded about their triumphs of faith.

Even in politics, it has only been a few years since women gained the right to vote in most of the industrialized world.

In the major part of the world today, societal norms and cultural standards repress female initiative, restricting them to one level or another of servitude, subordination, or of outright female subjugation.

From Moslem nations where women must cover their faces and bodies with long black flowing robes, to uncultured tribes where tradition relegates them to a status little above animals, the role of women is one of subservience and inferiority, and it should not be so.

Out of Context

Christian Church theology has extracted out of their medieval context five or six cultural admonitions made by Paul and by Peter and has construed those statements to establish perennial doctrinal absolutes which arbitrarily restrict women to silence in the church and that prohibit them from initiative and leadership in God's work.

This book can help you as a *Woman Without Limits,* to discover who you really are — that in God's eyes you are His special child, equal to anyone else in the world and designed by Him with unlimited potential.

For more than four decades my husband and I have proclaimed the gospel to millions, face to face, in over 70 nations.

My role as a woman in apostolic gospel ministry has been as unlimited as any man's ministry could be — and yours can be unlimited too.

It has been my privilege to organize our big crusades, to meet heads of state and government officials, to secure crusade permits, to contract stadiums and crusade grounds, to install equipment, to negotiate with businesses for tons of literature and to purchase thousands of tools for evangelism for follow-up distribution among *bona fide* national Christian women and men workers.

I have organized the co-operating pastors, set up the workers' institutes and convert schools, then presided over the mass crusades which we have conducted worldwide. And I always share with my husband in our preaching and teaching ministries, in addition to my own writing ministry.

My responsibilities as Chairperson of *OSFO International* places our USA world headquarters and all of our overseas offices under my charge, as well as the direction of our enormous world-wide missionary outreaches.

My husband and I are teammates. We share all aspects of our ministry. We are co-workers. We need each other, and we realize it. We fulfill each other. We are in love. We share our lives together.

T.L. and I function and minister on an equal basis in God's work because we are both called of God, we are both anointed, and we are both confirmed by the power of the Holy Spirit as Christ's messengers.

Being a woman does not limit me as a believer, as a disciple of Jesus Christ, as His follower, as His servant, as His witness, or as His ambassador.

What He said to all believers, He says to me — and to you also, if you are a woman. Never question that, and never allow any person, creed, doctrine or dogma to mitigate that fact.

Christ's Great Commission applies to women the same as it does to men.

The power of the Holy Spirit in a woman's life is no different than in a man's life.

The promises of Christ are for women the same as they are for men.

The gifts of the Holy Spirit function the same in a woman believer as in a man believer.

Since Jesus Christ redeemed all of humanity and sent back the Holy Spirit upon both women and men, gender is no longer a qualifying factor in God's work.

This book can help you discover who you are as a woman, and your unlimited potential in Jesus Christ.

New dimensions of ministry are within your grasp.

A New Lifestyle

A new life of victory and of unlimited accomplishment is before you as a woman.

A new style of living and a new self-image can

unfold for you.   You can see yourself like God
sees you, once the blinds of traditional theology are
removed from your eyes.

The miracle power of God can at last be as
unrestrained in you as it can be in any believing
man.

Success, achievement, love, status, beauty and a
new self-dignity can begin to unfold in your life.
But it can only happen if you as a woman, are ma-
ture enough to take a fresh look at life and to discover the secret of real success as a *Woman
Without Limits*.

Anointed by the Holy Spirit

Chosen of God

Commissioned by Jesus Christ

Proclaimer of good news worldwide

Chapter 43

THE ROLE OF GOD'S WOMAN

NOT LONG AGO, I had one of my many encounters with some of the traditional barriers which religion has set up to limit women in ministry.

I was delegated by the board of directors of *OSFO International* to visit an area abroad which had been almost unreached by the gospel. Church leaders in bordering districts were concerned and had appealed for our help in evangelizing this tough area.

Researching the facts confirmed that a valid and urgent need did exist.

We were prepared to finance the opening and establishing of new churches throughout the region, but the groundwork had to be done and the details worked out carefully so that the seed-idea of a great plan for God would not be aborted.

The Problem: I Was a Woman

Upon my arrival, a church bishop, together with a delegation of pastors, met me at the airport. They had graciously prepared a program for me. But I observed that their scheduled activities had nothing to do with the mission I was there to accomplish.

Since I believe that every problem contains the

seed of its own solution, I tuned in to God for a quick discovery of the seed in this one. I certainly did not want to offend a bishop.

Without reacting to their program, I began to list all the things that had to be done before we could proceed with their program. The problem: The things I had listed could only be done (according to them) by a man. It would be a serious violation of their church's doctrine for me, a woman, to act in such a role of leadership.

The solution: I realized that I would have to approach this unreached area via government channels instead of through the biased religious hierarchy. It worked.

I was graciously accepted by government agencies, in my official capacity as chief executive officer of *OSFO International*, and my being a woman did not cause a single national official to even bat an eye.

Once the cooperation and blessing of the governor, the tribal king and the village chiefs was evident, all of the pastors gave full support and we were able to leave no stone unturned. The gospel invasion was carried out victoriously. My mission was accomplished, and another bishop was added to my long list of cherished clergymen friends who have accepted me in my role, observing that God is not limited in a woman believer.

Chapter 44

WOMAN'S ROLE IN THE FALL AND IN REDEMPTION

EVE, THE FIRST WOMAN God created[1] has inspired many a discourse which has resulted in ironclad church doctrines that put women (as they say) "in their place," silent and non-assertive in public ministry for our Lord.

If a woman's disobedience should be emphasized as the reason for the fall of the human race, it is equally appropriate to emphasize that it was a woman's obedience that resulted in the redemption of humankind.

In fact, that may be why God gave the world the Savior through the obedience of a woman — to illustrate forever that women are redeemed and restored to their original position of equality with men just as when God created them both in His own image. *Let us make humankind in our image ...; and let them have complete authority ...*[2]

Women in Redemption

God chose a woman as His channel for redemption, forgiveness and eternal salvation. A woman was used to bring joy, peace, love, comfort and fulfillment to the human race.[3]

Women were active in the ministry of Jesus.[4]

To portray the *Woman Without Limits* in teamwork with Christ, there is no better example than Mary of Magdala, a demon-possessed business woman.

1. She came to Jesus.

2. She was delivered by Him.

3. She became His follower and supporter.

4. She assisted in the business arrangements of His itineraries.

5. She was at the cross.

6. She helped prepare His body for burial.

7. She was there when Jesus arose from the dead.

8. She was visited by Christ after He arose.

9. She received His message.

10. She delivered His message to the apostles.

11. We can be sure that she was filled with the Holy Ghost on the Day of Pentecost.

12. She was obviously an anointed messenger and witness of Jesus Christ in the early church.

There are at least six facts about Mary Magdalene that offer hope and courage to every woman who purposes to follow and to obey Christ. We shall look at these facts in the following chapters.

1.   Ge.3:20   3.   Lu.1:26-38
2.   Ge.1:26AB   4.   Lu.8:1-3

Chapter 45

THE DEMON POSSESSED WOMAN

FIRST: MARY MAGDALENE had seven demons.

Since the number seven symbolizes completeness in Biblical text, we might say that Mary of Magdala was completely possessed of evil.

Demons do terrible things to people. A beautiful individual, under satanic influence, will commit sins otherwise unimaginable.

Those sins lead to captivity, mental anguish, sickness and torment.

Remember, *the thief (Satan) comes only to steal, and to kill and to destroy.*[1] That is what demons were doing to Mary. But Jesus cast those evil spirits from her so that she could have real life, abundant life.

The Jesus-Life for Women

The life that Jesus gives is clean, useful, happy, healthy, full of faith, hope and love. Instead of doing destructive things, the life that Jesus gives inspires you to do constructive and productive things.

Jesus delivers from bad habits that contaminate

the body, the mind and the spirit. He causes people to develop habits that help to cleanse and purify themselves as well as other habits that save life instead of destroying it.

That is what Jesus did for Mary who had been possessed of those seven demons. That is what He is still doing for women — and men today who are in need of His deliverance.

Three Wise Men

In one of our crusades, three handsome young men flew for ten hours from Europe, to attend the meetings and to witness what God was doing among the multitudes of people who were attending.

Two beautiful young women (prostitutes) saw them in town, followed them to their hotel and made every possible attempt to allure the handsome young visitors to their rooms.

But the fellows were real Christians — involved in soulwinning ministries among the chemically dependents and the prostitutes in Europe. They knew how to present Christ to these girls.

The result: both ladies attended the crusade, heard the gospel message, were saved and transformed by Christ. They were referred to one of the local pastors who welcomed them to church. They learned rapidly and became strong Christians and faithful members.

Later in another of our crusades, that pastor attended with a group from his church. Those young women were among them. They had become

stalwart Christians, and now they have become living examples of the transforming power of Christ,
witnessing and sharing His life with others.

Jesus Christ came to those young girls like He
came to Mary Magdalene. He delivered them like
he delivered her. They began to follow Him like
she did.

That is what can happen to you. You may not
be possessed of seven demons. But whatever your
need is, Jesus is coming to you — right now,
through this book, and before you have finished
reading it, your life can be identified with Him in
a new way. You can become a *Woman Without
Limits,* in teamwork with Christ.

1.   Jn.10:10RSV

"As Jesus was teaching, ... the power of the Lord was present to heal them." Lu. 5:17 Daisy believes that the Lord desires to heal those who suffer, if they believe His promises which she proclaims to them. "The Lord sent His word and healed them" Ps. 107:20

Chapter 46

TRANSFORMATION OF A MARKED WOMAN

SECOND: MARY MAGDALENE was completely delivered.

Her hate was turned to love, her suffering to peace, her torment to confidence, her sickness to health, her sorrow to joy, her failure to success; instead of shame she had honor and respect.

Jesus took the good in Mary — her God-given abilities, and made her a useful, successful person. She became a minister to human needs. According to respected Bible commentaries, she was on Jesus' team as He went from village to village.[1]

Jesus came to redeem women the same as men, and to identify with them as His co-workers, His disciples, His messengers, His representatives — the same as He identifies with men.

Since religious tradition and culture has so restricted women to subservient roles, historians very rarely recorded their courageous acts of faith.

But the New Testament clearly portrays women in places of great influence and action, carrying out the new role of the new redeemed *Woman Without Limits.*

There is deliverance for every woman on earth

— not only deliverance from the chains and bondage of demons and sin, but there is freedom from the fetters and enslavement of religious tradition that has sentenced her to silence and has quarantined her within the scrupulous limits imposed by outdated theological dogmas.

A Woman and Christ Can Do Anything

When Jesus becomes the Master of your life, you as a woman can do anything that God puts in your heart to do.

According to Bible scholars, Mary had a keen, innate business propensity and was a highly skilled woman. Scholars say that her madness was periodic; that in her rational times, she gained wealth through her unusual business acumen. The devil tried to destroy her talent, but Jesus transformed her life. She became one of the pillars in His ministry.

Dr. Henry H. Halley says in his renowned Bible Handbook that "Mary Magdalene was the most prominent and outstanding leader among women. She is named more than any of the others ... a woman of some wealth ... a woman of unblemished character ... the leading woman of Jesus' group ... at the head of (His) religious work." (Pages 503-504).

Mary and other women went ahead of Jesus to make necessary preparations for Him and the other members of His team.

Mary Magdalene was grateful for her new life and showed her gratitude by being involved in Jesus'

ministry.   She is named as having *ministered to
Christ of her substance.*[2]   That is a beautiful pic-
ture of a *Woman Without Limits,* in teamwork with
Christ.

Deliverance From Chauvinism

I have a friend who is the wife of a prominent
pastor.

Until she attended one of our national conferences, she was timid, non-expressive and did little
more in the church than to warm one of the pews.

Her husband was revolutionized by our mes-
sages.   He saw how his own male superiority complex had made no allowance for his wife's ministry
to develop.   Her potential was totally uncultivated.

As a successful pastor, my friend's husband
was inundated by calls to preach and to minister.
He drove himself day and night, almost to the
breaking point, while his allegiance to archaic religious tradition kept his wife's powerful personality
and energy shackled and restrained.

They both got their eyes opened during the
course of our conference teaching.

Our pastor friend saw the terrible waste of
human energy, influence and talent that church tradition had sanctioned by keeping the women of his
great congregation in silence.

His wife realized how ridiculous it had been
for her to allow herself to be subdued and subjugated by outdated chauvinistic dogmas and prejudice.

She had actually retired within herself and had lost her drive for winning souls to Christ.

In our conference, I preached about how Jesus delivered Mary Magdalene — not only from demons, but from the Jewish tradition that had limited women to subservient roles.

Fruit of Freedom

That couple was delivered — he from his religious chauvinism, and she from her docile capitulation to man's traditional demeaning dogmas concerning women.

That woman, with the encouragement of her revolutionized soulwinning husband, began to awaken to the fact that she, as a woman, was filled with the Holy Ghost, the same as her husband; that she had the same anointing, the same faculties and the same responsibility to share Jesus with her world as her husband had.

She not only became a powerful voice and influence in their rapidly growing church organization, but she began to organize the women of her area.

Today, under that dynamic woman's leadership, they have birthed a women's organization of women-preachers, women-evangelists, women-church-builders, women-convention-conductors, women-community-promoters, women-home-builders, women-school and clinic-organizers, and they have now been given a prize piece of property where they have dedicated their national women's headquarters building and teaching center. They have done it in such good taste that even the government is recognizing their influence and contribution to society.

God's Worldwide Corps of Women Soulwinners

I pray that every woman who reads this book will have a miracle deliverance — not only from sin, disease and negativism, but also from the traditions of churchmen that keep God's corps of women in a restricted domain of silence and of insignificance.

This official ecclesiastical suppression of women in the church has been a great convenience for pious ladies who lack drive, zeal and courage for God's work.

How convenient it is for acquiescent and docile women to excuse themselves, parroting: "But I am a woman and I am to be silent."

Pious men in the church love to placate and cajole such women — as long as they remain silent, submissive and subservient.

Never forget: Strong men welcome the potency and the creative energy of strong women.

Successful men value the influence and the constructive imagination of competent women.

Only weak men feel threatened by the skills or logistics of capable women.

Only fragile and anemic men react negatively to the participation of qualified women in posts of influence and of leadership.

The gospel must be proclaimed by every voice and instrument possible. Christ's commission is addressed to all believers, both female and male. The church can no longer afford to silence two-thirds of her constituency because of gender discrimination.

Mary became a *Woman Without Limits,* in teamwork with Christ, and that is what God invites you to become today.

1.   Lu.8:1-3
2.   Lu.8:3

Chapter 47

WOMEN IN CHRIST'S MINISTRY

THIRD: MARY MAGDALENE became a follower of Jesus. She was one of His disciples.

Mary sat at Christ's feet as a learner[1] — and she did this in an epoch when Jewish rabbinic tradition held that it was better "for the words of Torah to be destroyed by fire than to be imparted to women". (Pg.179. *Every Man's Talmud*)

Jesus totally contravened this Jewish attitude when He commended Mary who *sat at His feet, and heard His word,*[2] and when *He went through every city and village, preaching and bringing the glad tidings,* with *certain women ... and many other women,* in His company, who obviously *heard* His teachings and *learned* His word.[3]

Study Jesus' life and ministry. He never did or said anything to infer that women are to be His subjugated, inferior, nonexpressive followers.

Women were taught by Christ and have been redeemed by Him, to be His witnesses, His disciples, His co-workers, and His anointed messengers, the same as men.[4]

Women were a vital part of Jesus' life and ministry then, and they are vital to His plan in this generation.

Jesus said: *My mother and my brothers and*

sisters are these who are hearing and doing the word of God.[5] Jesus used the word *adelphos,* which was translated in the King James version of the Bible as simply "brothers", but which is used 30 times in Acts and 130 times in Paul's writings to distinctly mean "brothers and sisters," people of both sexes.

Put Yourself in the Scriptures

When you read the gospels of Matthew, Mark, Luke and John, the teachings of Jesus will come alive to you as a woman, by putting your name in the scriptures. Say "woman" and "she" in place of "man" and "he."

The Bible traditionally uses the words "man" and "brethren" when the meaning is understood by all scholars to clearly designate "humankind" and "all believers".

Once you as a woman, learn to see yourself and to include yourself in God's word, then you will pray with greater faith and intimacy, and the Lord will talk to you. You will learn to let Him speak to you as a woman, through His word, and as you listen, you will hear His voice.

Ideas will come to you. Thoughts will enter your mind, sent from your Lord as messages to you. You will experience His guidance. It is a wonderful experience. Do it daily and a very personal relationship will develop between you and your Lord and Master, Jesus.

This is the only way the *Woman Without Limits* can discover success, achievement and fulfillment in the work and ministry of Christ.

Teen-Age Village Girl
Preaching to Multitudes

A young girl was converted in Africa.   She has become one of our very personal friends.

She loves Jesus and is sensitive to His Spirit.

She wanted to work for Him and to be an evangelist.   But people scoffed at her.   She was a girl.   Girls could not preach.   Girls must become brides.   They were worth a good price to their fathers who would collect a good dowry for their marriage.

Day and night this girl yearned to tell others about Jesus.

One night she dreamed a dream.   She saw her crippled grandmother.   She laid her hands on her and the old paralyzed woman was miraculously healed.

Was it just a dream, or was it prophetic guidance like when Paul saw the man in Macedonia who pleaded, *Come over ... and help us?*[6]

Should this young African lady regard the idea that came into her mind, through this unusual dream, as if God were speaking to her and leading her in Christian ministry?

The Doers and the Non-Doers

You see, there are only two classes of Christians: Some get ideas and do nothing about them; others get ideas and act on them, and they become successful in Christian ministries.

This girl got an idea from an overwhelming
dream, and she acted upon it. She went to her
grandmother just as she had dreamed; she laid her
hands on the old paralyzed woman in the name of
Jesus, and the miracle took place. The woman
was miraculously healed.

Then it occurred to the young lady that she
could do the same to others. So she acted on that
idea too. More miracles took place.

She realized that God had called her to minister to the needs of hurting people. She obeyed.
Soon she was preaching to hundreds, then thousands,
then tens of thousands of people, and praying for
these masses.

She was just a native Kikuyu tribesgirl, but
God was confirming her simple ministry of proclaiming Christ, with marvelous miracles, and hundreds of conversions were taking place.

What a paradox! What an affront to theological
tradition in Africa! A teen-age Kikuyu village girl
was preaching to multitudes and was leading thousands of souls to Christ!

That girl is a teamworker with Christ. She is
truly a *Woman Without Limits*.

Canadian Woman Evangelized Millions

Aimee Semple McPherson was a young woman
from the prairies of western Canada.

She set out to preach Christ. It was not easy.
She was persecuted and criticized by theologians
everywhere. She was a woman. Tradition held
that she should not preach; she should be silent —
whether souls were going to hell or not.

But Aimee had a vision. She had a call, and
she paid the price to obey that call and to be
Christ's messenger and co-worker in reaching millions with the gospel confirmed by miracles.

In religion, rules and traditions are so often
given greater importance than life and deliverance.

Women Unlimited in God's Work

I have heard my husband say so often: "If it
is wrong for women who are concerned about lost
souls to preach the gospel and to get people saved
and healed and blessed, then let them do it anyway,
and let God lay their sin to my charge."

I've heard him say, "I do not believe that God
will become angry with any woman for doing what
Jesus told all believers to do: 'Go preach the
gospel to every creature.' I do not think God will
punish any woman for proclaiming the good news to
the world, for getting souls saved, for building
churches, or for doing anything a woman is inspired
or led of God to do in private or public ministry."

It was not easy for Aimee Semple McPherson
to load her family and their scanty belongings in an
old Model-T Ford touring car and cross the western desert, to carry the gospel of healing and salvation to the new California frontier.

Woman Evangelist Faces
Opposition by Clergy

The burning heat, the dusty roads and the rigors of desert travel in the twenties should have been enough for brave Aimee to sustain. After all, she had lost her young missionary husband in China.

But it is never easy for a woman to achieve success in the ministry. Aimee not only had to cope with the heartbreak of loneliness, and the rigors of travel in that epoch, but she had to confront the storms of religious opposition to her ministry of mercy — opposition to her for being a woman, a woman preacher, a woman evangelist, a woman church builder.

Despite almost every barrier and difficulty that Satan's cunning could conceive in order to obstruct her ministry, that courageous woman reached some of the greatest crowds in the history of American evangelism, and brought peace, healing miracles and salvation to multitudes of people in Christ's name.

Tens of thousands of souls were brought to Christ in the historic crusades which Aimee McPherson so bravely conducted, and were added to the churches of that epoch.

She was a vessel signally anointed by the Holy Spirit. She was in teamwork with Christ!

Maintaining Female Discrimination

Ever since God poured out His Holy Spirit upon the women as well as upon the men[7] He intended to use them in the same way that He uses men.[8]

But Jewish heritage and culture predominated in the apostolic era. The new Christian churches were permeated with the bias of gender discrimination which tradition had imposed upon women for centuries.

These newly formed communities of believers were inclined to incorporate and to embrace as much Jewish tradition as possible. They continued to keep women in the background, and little was ever recorded of the faith exploits and gospel ministries of those heroic and courageous women believers in the early church who paid such exorbitant and brutal prices for their faith.

Mary Magdalene's life-experience contradicted Jewish tradition, and Jesus approved and endorsed her contradiction of rabbinic rules, by teaching her and *many other women* the principles of the kingdom of God.[9]

Mary became a follower of Jesus — an imitator of His life and ministry — and an avid learner of His teachings.

Jesus said, *As my Father has sent Me, even so I send you.*[10] That includes every woman who chooses to live her life in teamwork with Christ, the same as it included those New Testament women who made such sacrifices to follow Him.

1. Lu.10:39,42
2. Lu.10:39
3. Lu.8:1-3
4. Lu.23:27,49,55; 24:10;
    Mk.15:41;
    Ac.5:14; 8:3,12; 13:50; 16:13; 17:4,12; 22:4
5. Lu.8:21 - Wuest
6. Ac.16:9
7. Ac.1:14; 2:4
8. Ac.5:14,12; 13:50; 17:4,12
9. Lu.8:1-3
10. Jn.20:21

"Mary Magdalene became a follower of Jesus, an imitator of His life and ministry and an avid learner of His teachings; and any woman can do the same."

Chapter 48

WOMEN AS CHRIST'S PARTNERS

FOURTH: MARY MAGDALENE became a partner in Jesus' ministry.

Mary, Joanna (the wife of King Herod's business manager) and Susanna are women named in the gospels as some of those who *contribut(ed) from their private means to the support of Jesus and His disciples.*[1]

Those women had been healed, delivered and blessed by Jesus' teaching and they learned to share with Him in ministering both to His needs, and to the needs of others.

Those women expressed in a material way their gratitude to Christ. They made it possible for His ministry to reach more and more people. They chose to be partners in His ministry, and He sanctioned their partnership.

Those women had heard the parable of the sower and had grasped the truth which Jesus had emphasized. They had learned well the lesson of giving and of receiving.[2]

Mary had heard and believed Jesus' message: *Give, and it shall be given to you.*[3] She had sown and she had reaped.

Mary was a giver! And Mary prospered.

As a follower of Jesus, that is among the first lessons to be learned in order to enjoy a fulfilled, happy life of plenty as a *Woman Without Limits.*

God wants a host of Mary Magdalenes today — enterprising women who can build businesses into great successes, producing high profits so that God's work can be financed worldwide.

The Asian Businesswoman

A young woman was converted in one of our Asian crusades. She had a desire to spread the gospel to others.

She studied her Bible and began sharing Jesus with people. Then she suddenly had a bright idea: Form a business and make money, then use the profits to organize and finance soulwinning projects and outreaches.

The more she planted her profits in God's work, the more her business grew. Soon she had a chain of businesses.

Like Mary Magdalene, she used her business talent to become a partner in the ministry of Christ. Not only has she become an effective preacher, evangelist and Bible teacher herself, but her business abilities have developed a powerful initiative for evangelism — not only in her country but in reaching across her borders into neighboring countries through her gospel outreaches.

She pondered the traditional enterprising effi-

ciency of other Asian women as they accumulated
riches for their private families. She wanted to
develop her enterprise to further God's work.

What a wonderful concept for a believing
woman! What an affront to Christian theological
tradition in Asia that still shackles and stifles
women in submissive and subservient roles within
the Church.

That woman has broken all of those discriminating rules and has chosen to let Christ work
through her as a *Woman Without Limits*.

By using her good sense and by acting on
Christ's word to all believers, that Asian woman is
not only financing successful soulwinning outreaches, but she herself has become a dynamic
woman preacher in Asia. Her idea has worked.

A worldwide ministering corps of such women
is on the increase; women who are anointed by the
Holy Spirit and who are doing God's work on a
grand scale.

That is God's *Woman Without Limits,* in
teamwork with Christ.

No Limits for Women of God

Women, anointed by God's spirit can do anything men can do in God's work and they should
never be limited or restrained because of their
color or their gender.

In today's world, women chauffeur trucks and
buses, operate machinery, weld steel, pilot air-

planes, captain ships, direct conglomerates; women
are entrepreneurs, doctors, teachers, lawyers,
judges, politicians; women are governors, senators,
judges, provincial commissioners, presidents and
prime ministers of nations.

What a waste for religious tradition to repress
this enormous world-wide human resource and to
restrict women believers to silence in the public
ministry of the Church!

If men can create organizations, form businesses, and build enterprises, women can too — and
they are doing it throughout the world.

If men can rent halls, hire auditoriums, lease
stadiums and mount tents for evangelism, women
can too.

If men can invent and create, so can women.
If men can manage business affairs, so can women.

If men can preach and win souls, train converts, build churches, establish denominations or
fellowships, found Bible schools, ordain men and
women for Gospel ministries, appoint pastors, ad-
minister organizations, and commission missionaries, women can too.

In today's world, women are taking their places
in business and on the labor force alongside men —
in shipyards, oil industries, factories; in science,
politics, and even in the army, the navy, and the air
force. Women are competent in every field of expertise, from machinists to astronauts.

Women can fill any role or position or ministry

Women can fill any role or position or ministry in the Church that any man can fill if they prepare themselves and if they allow Christ and the Holy Spirit to be unlimited in them.

It is time for women of God to come down from their feminine pedestals and to take up their crosses as Christ's followers and witnesses — cost whatever it may cost in money or physical effort or religious opposition or persecution.

It is time for women to engage themselves in the ministry for which the Holy Spirit rests upon them — witnessing of Jesus Christ and sharing Him with their world.

Women, like Mary Magdalene, were full partners in Christ's work then, and He expects women who follow Him to be full partners in His work today.

You can be a *Woman Without Limits*, in teamwork with Christ.

Take your place and do exploits in His name.

1.   Lu.8:2-3LB
2.   Lu.6:38
3.   Lu.6:38

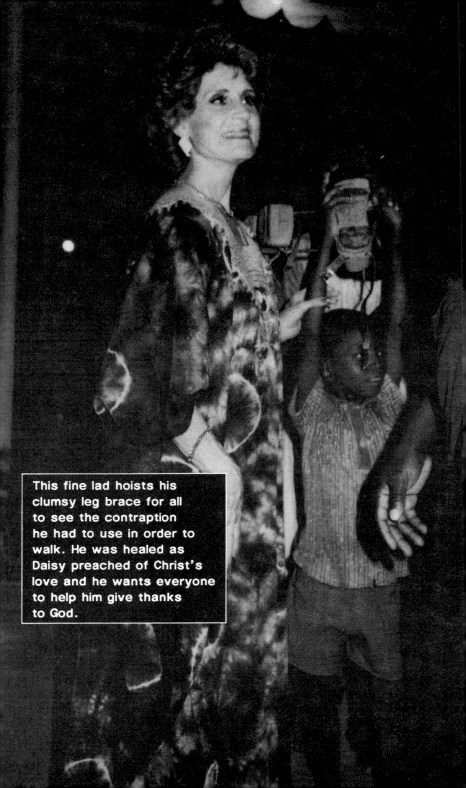

This fine lad hoists his clumsy leg brace for all to see the contraption he had to use in order to walk. He was healed as Daisy preached of Christ's love and he wants everyone to help him give thanks to God.

Chapter 49

WOMAN MESSENGER

FIFTH: MARY MAGDALENE proclaimed Christ's message.

The most basic message of our Christian faith is the resurrection of Jesus from the dead. That fact separates Christianity from all religions and makes it a reality instead of a ritual.

Amazing as it may seem, a woman was the first person to proclaim that great message.

It is significant that Jesus trusted a woman and, in fact, commissioned her to proclaim the first message of His resurrection — and to proclaim it to the men.

Jesus was making it very clear that the redemption of humankind at the cross had restored womanhood to her original place of equality in God's plan.

Women and Men Equal in Christ

In the beginning God created humankind — male and female, equal before Him.

Jesus, through His life, death and resurrection redeemed humankind — male and female, equally.

Women and men alike have access to God once again on an individual and equal basis, with Jesus as their mediator.[1]

As Paul said, *We are no longer Jews or Greeks or slaves or free men or even men or women, but we are all the same ... we are one in Christ Jesus.*[2]

Women, as well as men, may now be filled and anointed with the same power of the same Holy Spirit, for the same purpose and for the same ministry — to witness of Jesus Christ and to proclaim His gospel to every creature, in all the world.

Sex discrimination in Christ's ministry is simply unfounded in God's redemptive plan.

To indelibly underscore this point, Jesus sent a woman whom He had delivered from demons, to announce the powerful message of the resurrection to the apostles themselves.

What a challenge for women today!

What is preaching? My husband defines it as: Telling what you know about Jesus. He says that when a Christian does that, and incorporates some Bible verses to substantiate what is said, that is the greatest preaching on earth.

Sharing Christ's Message

St. Francis of Assisi suggested to his friends: "Let us go into the village and preach the gospel."

As they set out on foot, St. Francis was poised and unperturbed as he went about counseling travelers, conversing with people, lending a hand to those

in need, helping those with problems, showing love
to the needy, friendship to the lonely, and compassion to the unfortunate, touching, praying, talking, counseling or blessing each one whom he en-
countered.

The day passed and the group was returning
home. A disciple expressed: "Master, we set out
to preach the gospel to the people; the day has
passed, and not a single sermon has been delivered."

St. Francis replied: "Oh, but yes! We have
been preaching the gospel the whole day."

On another occasion St. Francis of Assisi said:
"Preach the gospel all the time, and if necessary,
even use words."

So in this sense, Mary Magdalene, a woman
partner in teamwork with Christ was a proclaimer
of the good news of the Kingdom.

Mary told what Jesus had done for her and she
delivered His message. That is preaching the
Gospel.

So — why should women not preach and teach
the gospel? If the Bible is to be accepted and
obeyed by all believers, then women and men alike
(all believers) are commissioned by Christ to *go ...
to all the world, and preach the gospel to every creature.*[3]

That is teamwork with Christ.

Women believers constitute Christ's body and
His church the same as men do.

Women believers constitute Christ's body and
His church the same as men do.

Teamwork with Christ for women was made
possible on the day of Pentecost. With the sins of
humanity having been remitted and expunged forever,
any person regardless of age, race, color, economic
status or gender, who believes on Jesus Christ and
who receives Him as Lord and Savior is justified
and is restored back to God's side as His partner
and friend.

Barriers or divisions or separations or discriminations are no longer legitimate between men
or women,[4] bond or free,[5] Jews or Gentiles,[6]
clergy or laiety.[7]

All who accept Christ as Saviour and Lord are
His witnesses. All are His representatives, His
ambassadors, His voice, His hands, His messengers, His body. They all — both men and women
— are to proclaim the message that He is risen.
That is what you and I are saved to do.

So often in our ministry together, my husband
and I have had the great joy of seeing women (men
too, of course) come to Christ just like Mary Magdalene did, and then parallel her life-style as disciples of Jesus.

Once a Prostitute — Now a Pastor

In one of our mass crusades abroad, a woman
prostitute accepted Christ. She had been a cast-

away, abandoned because she was dying of cancer. With no hope of life, no knowledge of true love and no faith in God, she was brought to our crusade.

She listened as we related the account of God's plan of redemption.   She believed and accepted Jesus Christ into her heart.   Her eyes became a fountain of tears that bathed her face.

She said, "Oh, I feel so clean.   I feel like a virgin again.   That awful guilt of sin is gone.   I feel so free, so light, so wonderful."

Then she asked: "What can I do to show Jesus I love Him and that I am His follower?"

We told her to do what every believer was commanded to do:

1) Tell others what Jesus has done for you;

2) Learn Biblical verses that substantiate your experience and quote them;

3) Tell people that Christ will do the same for them.

Every week she grew in the Lord and before long that woman, healed of cancer and transformed by the life of Christ, was spending her time doing what we had counseled her to do, preaching and telling about Jesus to others.

Then the inevitable happened.   She had led many people to Christ and she felt a responsibility to help them more.   She came back for counsel.

We assured her that she could gather them together and teach them all at one time.

That solved her problem.

The result? She and her converts kept expanding their outreaches and leasing larger facilities. Soon a strong soulwinning church with nearly a thousand members developed under her leadership. She became a great pastor, simply because she did not know that a woman was not supposed to do such things. She taught each new believer what she had learned:

1) Tell others what Jesus has done for you.

2) Quote scriptures to verify it.

3) Tell people that Christ will do the same for them.

Any woman (or any man) who has received Jesus Christ as Lord, is not only authorized, but is commissioned by Him to do those things. And there can be no more authentic ministry in the Christian Church than doing that. Any woman believer can be in teamwork with Christ as a *Woman Without Limits*.

Who Is Lord? Paul or Christ?

If the institutionalized Church requires you as a woman, to be *silent* within their walls, never allow that to discourage you. Go out to your world where the people live and work and play. That is where there is the greatest need for your message of good news. After all, most of the people within the church walls have already heard of Jesus Christ. Outside the church is where a hurting world needs His ministry of love.

The Bible says: *The field is the world.*[8]

No woman believer should feel deprived if she is prohibited from speaking inside the church building. The ministry and message of God's woman counts most out where the people are.*

Rather than for a woman to complain about the limited domains where she is restricted and stifled, let the *Woman Without Limits* lift up her eyes and look on the fields of the whole free world, out where neither theological tradition nor Paul's alleged restrictions apply any limits whatsoever to her ministry in teamwork with Christ. Out there she is completely free to minister as Christ's witness and as His authorized representative.

If you feel obliged to observe Paul's alleged restraints inside of the church sanctuary, should you not feel equally obliged to obey your Lord Jesus Christ outside of the church sanctuary? Should you give greater credence to Paul (even if his words applied to women of today's culture) than you give to Christ who is your Lord?

We should remember that great scholars agree that the ideas concerning women, expressed by Paul and Peter, have been greatly exaggerated beyond their contextual intent; that they were never expressed as general dictums for women of all ages;

---

*Get my husband's two books, *SOULWINNING* and *OUTSIDE THE SANCTUARY*, both of which deal with this subject.

but that they were written as guidelines for new women believers in a precarious and menacing epoch for the new Christian Church.

Jesus said nothing about these alleged limitations. He commissioned women (along with men) to *preach the Gospel* as His *witnesses*. Should women acquiesce to what tradition imposes, and ignore what Jesus clearly commissioned them to do?

When Jesus commanded: *Go into all the world, and preach the gospel to every creature,* that commission was for every believer, regardless of color, race, culture or gender.

As a follower of Jesus, do what He told His followers to do — proclaim Christ's message. Be His witness. Act as His authorized representative, partner and co-worker.

1.	1 Ti.2:5	4.	Ga.3:27	7.	Re.1:6
2.	Ga.3:28 LB	5.	1 Co.12:13	8.	Mt.13:38
3.	Mk.16:15	6.	Ro.10:12		

Chapter 50

WOMEN ANOINTED TO WITNESS

SIXTH: MARY MAGDALENE was filled with the Holy Ghost, we may be certain, and was anointed to be Christ's witness.

There can be no doubt that Mary was at the prayer meeting in the Upper Room following the ascension of Jesus.

The Biblical record states that about 120 followers of Christ[1] obeyed His instructions *to tarry in the city of Jerusalem until you are endued with power from on high.*[2] Verse 13 of Acts, chapter one, enumerates the eleven male disciples and states that they were present, in prayer and supplication, *with the women* (v.14).

Could it be that many of the 120 who had gathered to pray, were *women?* Who were *the women* with whom the followers of Christ were gathered?

Lesly F. Massey, in his book *Women In The New Testament* says, "The group likely includes those who accompanied Jesus from Galilee[3] and those present at the cross[4] and at the grave.[5] It is clear that they were a recognized part of the ... group and that they witnessed the miraculous activities at Pentecost."

So often, when significant events concerning Christ were recorded, Mary Magdalene was there.

She was faithful. She was obviously committed to
Christ and to all that He represented.

Mary left Magdala to follow Jesus and to share
in ministry with His other disciples. She was with
Him to the end. She was at the trial in Pilate's
Hall and she was at the cross where Jesus was
crucified. She even helped to prepare His body for
burial.

Mary was at the sepulchre where Jesus was
entombed.

She had patience to stay near His body when
others gave up and abandoned hope. She remained
loyal to the Lord when others denied Him.

Mary heard Him say that He would rise again.
Evidently she never forgot His words.

Mary searched for her Lord. She did not take
another's word; and she resisted the doubts of others. Why? Because she had faith. She had heard
Jesus teach.[6] Her faith had come by hearing His
word.[7]

Mary was there near the sepulchre when Christ
appeared. Her faithfulness paid off because she
heard Jesus call her by name.

Jesus revealed Himself in a special, personal
way to Mary. Then He commissioned her to tell
the men that He was alive again.

Those are reasons why we can be sure that
Mary Magdalene was there when the Holy Spirit
descended upon the believers.

This was another act of obedience and of faith in Christ's word.

Jesus had told them *not to depart from Jerusalem, but to wait for the Promise of the Father.*[8]

You can be sure that Mary of Magdala was one of *the women* present when the Holy Spirit descended, and that she was filled with the Holy Ghost, the same as the other women and men who were present, because Ac.2:4 says *they were all filled.* And her receiving this power had to be for the same purpose that men received this power.

You shall be witnesses to Me ... to the uttermost part of the earth.[9]

It would be difficult for a woman to fulfill this purpose, or to *prophesy* as Peter announced that the women would do,[10] and remain *silent.*

Mary, therefore, became one of the truly emancipated women, God's creation, redeemed, endued with power from on high and equipped to go anywhere as His witness.

The prophecy of Joel had been fulfilled.[11]

God began to pour out His *Spirit upon all flesh. His sons and His daughters began to prophesy,* and we can be sure that Mary was one of them.

1.	Ac.1:15	4.	Lu.23:27	8.	Ac.1:4 LB
2.	Lu.24:49	5.	Lu.24:10,22;	9.	Ac.1:8
3.	Mt.27:55;		Jn.20:1,11-18	10.	Ac.2:17
	Mk.15:41;	6.	Lu.18:31-33	11.	Jl.2:28
	Lu.23:49,55	7.	Ro.10:17		

"The new woman in the new church is the Woman Without Limits. Accept no suggestions promulgated by religion or culture, which contradict your position as a divine daughter in God's royal family."

Chapter 51

THE NEW WOMAN FOR THE NEW CHURCH

A NEW DAY DAWNED when Jesus came. He came for women and for men alike.

We can all have Christ's new life — both women and men who believe on Him.

We can all have hope — women as well as men who embrace Jesus as Lord.

We all have real purpose in living — women the same as men who are aware that Christ lives.

We have liberty. We are no longer slaves. We are no longer limited. We have been set free. Why? Because we are loved. We are needed. We are part of Christ's church. We are members of His Body. He is depending on us. Our world is depending on us — women the same as men.

Realize this and your life as a woman, will be changed in a wonderful way.

The new woman in the new church is the *Woman Without Limits*. She is not condemned but she is redeemed. Instead of living in torment, she lives in peace. In place of confusion, she has divine guidance. Her sickness has been replaced by God's health. Her poverty is turned into His prosperity.

Old enmities, hatred and jealousy are gone and the *Woman Without Limits* is filled with love, kindness, friendliness and gentleness.

Her failures have been changed to successes.

She is victorious!

Mary Magdalene is a symbol of what Jesus came to do. She exemplifies the *Woman Without Limits,* in teamwork with Christ.

At the resurrection, Christ defeated death, hell and the grave. He broke down the walls of division. He annulled the laws of segregation. He abolished the curse of racial or sexual discrimination.

In His death, burial and resurrection, Christ defeated Satan once and for all — for women as well as for men.

The new, liberated church was born.

The new woman in the new church emerged as a redeemed, spirit-filled, powerful woman to fill the role God created and destined her for.

The Choice Is Yours

Now every woman believer has a choice. She can choose to serve, to follow, to obey and to love her Lord, as Mary Magdalene did.

That is the choice I have made. I have chosen Jesus and the full, productive, active, dynamic life that He offers me. And He offers that life to every other woman believer the same as He offers it to every man believer.

What is your choice?

This is your moment of decision:

1. To accept Jesus into your life as your Savior and Lord;[1]

2. To become His follower in all things;[2]

3. To let Him love, serve and minister to people through you;[3]

4. To become involved in the Lord's work in whatever way you feel led of Him to serve;[4]

5. To become a sower, a giver, a reaper, an organizer, a producer, a minister;[5]

6. To pray earnestly and to listen for His answer to you personally;[6]

7. To be filled with the Holy Spirit so that you will have power to be His effective witness;[7]

8. To witness — to proclaim that Jesus is alive and that He is *the same yesterday, today and forever.*[8]

You are ready to make these choices.

You are ready to begin this new life, in teamwork with Christ, today.

The Key That Unlocks Life

It is vital to your life of success, that this new concept of you as a *Woman Without Limits,* be formed in you.   That is already happening in you through reading this book.

New dreams are being born in you.   A new consciousness of what God created you for and of your unlimited potential in Christ is being realized in you.

But your future, your new status, your new life of love, of happiness, of success, of achievement, and of self-respect all depend upon your willingness to make a decision right here and now, saying to yourself and to God: I will be a *Woman Without Limits,* in teamwork with Christ.

Your decision is the key that unlocks an exciting and successful new future for you.

You are no longer afraid to embark upon this new life of achievement with God.   You have come to realize that you can stand up to the repressive reaction that you may confront if you step out into the new role that God has designed for you.

Say to your Master: **Lord, here am I! Send me! Use Me! Show Yourself through me!**

Now is the time to put that decision on record before God.

Draw nigh to Him right now, and pray this prayer of commitment to Christ.

PRAYER

O Lord, I am Your child, created in Your image, with Your breath breathed into me.

I am a channel for Your Holy Spirit to work through — a human being for Christ to live in.

I have read good news in this book which you have caused to reach me.

I have looked up into the heavens, and I have had a new vision of myself in Your redemptive plan. I have dreamed a new dream.

I want, more than anything else in this world, to be Your instrument for good.

I am Your child, created for a unique purpose, and I am determined from this day, to allow Your dream to be fulfilled in my life.

O Lord Jesus, how marvelous to know what You did through Mary Magdalene! Now do Your will through me.

The demons that possessed Mary and tried to destroy her life have maneuvered to limit me too — demons of negativism and of fear, of poor self-image, of timidity and of inferiority, of subjection and of tradition. I resist and reject those demons and shall never give them power over me again. I thank You for driving them from me forever, because they can never live in me, now that You are my Lord.

Help me to discover all that I am in You, so that I shall never again bow to these negative influences that have restricted my usefulness in Your work and ministry.

Thank You for transforming my life, as You did Mary Magdalene's. Thank You that You have lifted me out of subjection and inferiority, and have put my feet on the road where there are no inferior beings, but where we are all equal before God, and where we can all be more than conquerors through Christ.

Thank You Lord, for calling me, like You called Mary Magdalene — and so many others.

I am Your follower. I am determined to be a faithful and committed Partner in Your ministry. I am restored! I receive You in my life.

From this moment, Your blood cleanses me. Your life is mine. My past is gone forever. I am anointed to witness to others.

My weaknesses and inferiorities, my defeats and denials of what You created me for, are gone forever. From today, I am a new member of Your new church!

I am saved! I am called by You! I am Your follower and fellow-worker! I am Yours and You are mine! Thank You for Your new life!

Truly, I am a NEW CREATURE in Christ Jesus! Thank you Lord. Amen.

1.	Ro.10:9,10	4.	Mt.4:19	7.	Ac.1:8
2.	Mt.16:24	5.	Lu.6:38	8.	He.13:8
3.	Mt.25:40	6.	Mt.7:7		

Chapter 52

UNLIMITED IN CHRIST

THE ONLY WAY Jesus Christ can be limited in a woman's life and ministry is if she chooses to limit Him by acquiescing in favor of cultural or religious traditions which circumscribe her expressions or activities in God's work.

Jesus said that religious people often *reject the commandment of God, that they may keep their own tradition,*[1] *Making the word of God of none effect.*[2]

The traditions of religion and culture limit women in ministry. Jesus does not.

Paul encourages all believers to have *knowledge of the Son of God, and to come to be a perfect* (a complete) *person, unto the measure of the stature of the fulness of Christ.*[3]

How big is Christ in you? What are the limits for the Holy Spirit at work in a woman? How spiritual is too spiritual for a woman? How much is too much, how big is too big, how far is too far for a woman? What are the limits for God's word if a woman acts upon them?

God was displeased with Israel when *they turned back and tempted God, and limited the Holy One.*[4]

For some, when they heard, did provoke: with whom He was grieved forty years. So we see that they could not enter in (to their promised land) *because of unbelief.*[5]

For a woman, this book has opened new horizons, new possibilities, new vistas and new fields of ministry as Christ's teammate. You as a woman, are *a partaker of the heavenly calling,*[6] and as you ponder your new lifestyle and ministry without limits, you will discover that questions, fears and trepidations will vanish as you *consider the Apostle and High Priest of your confession, Christ Jesus.*[7] Keep HIM only before you as your encourager, as your Lord, as your example.

You have become a partaker of Christ, if you hold the beginning of your confidence steadfast to the end.[8]

For it is God who works in you both to will and to do for His good pleasure,[9] so *let this mind be in you, which was also in Christ Jesus.*[10] Accept no thoughts or suggestions, proliferated by religion or by culture, which contradict your position as a divine daughter in God's royal family.

Cast down arguments and every high thing that exalts itself against the knowledge of God, bringing every thought into captivity to the obedience of Christ,[11] because you, like the early believers, have decided *to obey God rather than men.*[12]

As a woman believer and follower of Christ, and with Him at work in you, there are no legitimate limits for your ministry as His representative, either in private or in public.

See yourself as one of those *who loves God, and who is the called according to His purpose;* as one *whom He foreknew,* whom *He also predestined to be conformed to the image of His Son ... whom He called ... whom He justified* and whom *He also glorified.*[13]

Any woman who is foreknown by God and who is called, justified and glorified by Him, is a *Woman Without Limits.*   To limit her would be to limit Christ at work in her; it would be to limit the power of God's word and of His Holy Spirit, because of her gender.

To the woman who is a believer in Christ, He promises: *If you can believe, all things are possible to the one who believes.*[14]

* * *

PART III OF THIS BOOK talks about New Beginnings.   You as a woman, are facing new concepts, a new life pattern, new opportunities, new achievements, new self-esteem and new self-value.

Share these new blessings with other women. Place this, and my other books in their hands. Help them rise to the new level of a Jesus-woman, in teamwork with Christ — *without limits.*

Do not withhold good from those to whom it is due, when it is in the power of your hand to do so.[15]

1.	Mk.7:9	6.	He.3:1	11.	2Co.10:5
2.	Mk.7:13	7.	He.3:1	12.	Ac.5:29
3.	Ep.4:13	8.	He.3:14	13.	Ro.8:28-30
4.	Ps.78:41	9.	Ph.2:13	14.	Mk.9:23
5.	He.3:16,17,19KJV	10.	Ph.2:5	15.	Pr.3:27

ON THE GO LIFTING PEOPLE.

From their soulwinning youth, to their phenomenal success in world evangelism, T.L. and Daisy Osborn live their remarkable lives, ON THE GO, lifting people who need God's help, teaching millions that there are NO LIMITS of peace, of power, or of poise, when Jesus Christ is received and honored as LORD.